Popular politics in nineteenth-century England

WITHDRAWN

Popular Politics in Nineteenth-Century England provides an accessible introduction to the culture of English popular politics between 1815 and 1900, the period from Luddism to the New Liberalism. This is an area that has attracted great historical interest and has undergone fundamental revision in the last two decades. Did the Industrial Revolution create the working-class movement? Was liberalism (which transcended class divisions) the key mode of political argument?

Rohan McWilliam brings this central debate up to date for students of nineteenth-century British history. He assesses popular ideology in relation to the state, the nation, gender and the nature of party formation, and reveals a much richer social history emerging in the light of recent historiographical developments.

Rohan McWilliam is Lecturer in History at Anglia Polytechnic University, Cambridge.

Historical Connections

Series editors
Tom Scott *University of Liverpool*
Geoffrey Crossick *University of Essex*
John Davis *University of Connecticut*
Joanna Innes *Somerville College, University of Oxford*

Titles in the series

Popular politics in nineteenth-century England

Rohan McWilliam

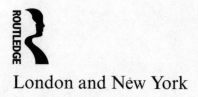

London and New York

First published 1998 by Routledge
11 New Fetter Lane, London EC4P 4EE

Simultaneously published in the USA and Canada
by Routledge
29 West 35th Street, New York, NY 10001

© 1998 Rohan McWilliam

Typeset in Times by Routledge
Printed and bound in Great Britain by
Clays Ltd, St Ives PLC

British Library Cataloguing in Publication Data
A catalogue record for this book is available from the British Library

Library of Congress Cataloging in Publication Data
A catalogue record for this book has been requested

ISBN 0–415–18675–7 (hbk)
ISBN 0–415–10841–1 (pbk)

In memory of my niece
ELSPETH MONICA McWILLIAM-BAGLEY

Contents

Series editors' preface

Historical Connections is a series of short books on important historical topics and debates, written primarily for those studying and teaching history. The books offer original and challenging works of synthesis that will make new themes accessible, or old themes accessible in new ways, build bridges between different chronological periods and different historical debates, and encourage comparative discussion in history.

If the study of history is to remain exciting and creative, then the tendency towards fragmentation must be resisted. The inflexibility of older assumptions about the relationship between economic, social, cultural and political history has been exposed by recent historical writing, but the impression has sometimes been left that history is little more than a chapter of accidents. This series will insist on the importance of processes of historical change, and it will explore the connections within history: connections between different layers and forms of historical experience, as well as connections that resist the fragmentary consequences of new forms of specialism in historical research.

Historical Connections will put the search for these connections back at the top of the agenda by exploring new ways of uniting the different strands of historical experience, and by affirming the importance of studying change and movement in history.

Geoffrey Crossick
John Davis
Joanna Innes
Tom Scott

Acknowledgements

Whilst I bear sole responsibility for the contents of this book, I have benefited immensely from the support and criticism of others. Malcolm Chase, Matthew Cragoe, James Epstein, Robert Gray, Simon Gunn, Michelle Hawley, Matthew Hendley, David Nash and Frank Trentmann all gave up time to read portions of the manuscript. My thanks go to the editorial board of the 'Historical Connections' series and particularly to Geoffrey Crossick who not only invited me to write the book but has provided me with characteristically acute comments. I also thank Heather McCallum at Routledge for her patience with a book that must have looked as though it would never arrive. My parents I hope know how much I treasure their love and support. The final debt is to my wife and fellow historian, Kelly Boyd. Commenting on the manuscript was the least of her contribution.

Full publication details are only supplied for works published since 1945.

Introduction

This is a study of the culture of English popular politics between 1815 and 1900. Principally concerned with political identity, it will argue that the investigation of ideas should not be divorced from social context or experience. This is an area that since the Second World War has attracted immense historical interest but which has recently undergone a great deal of change. The purpose of this book is to introduce readers to new debates in the field and to suggest ways in which it might be developed further.

The title is apparently simple, covering the period from Luddism to the New Liberalism, but it needs to be unpacked. I deliberately use the term 'popular politics' as opposed to 'working-class' politics because many political ideas were not peculiar to one class or another but were trans-class. Although I persist in believing that class was a fundamental form of social identity in the nineteenth century, this book holds that a narrow focus on class consciousness is not a sufficient explanation for the form and language of politics because there were other kinds of social identity that were often equally important. For example, Chapter Five examines the ways in which popular politics can be seen as a series of debates about the meaning of the constitution. The 'nineteenth century' of the title is perhaps not satisfactory as this study looks back to the defining experiences of the 1790s and also forward to 1914 (as well as to the politics of the recent past). Given the lengthy time span, this book does not purport to be exhaustive in treatment. Instead, it focuses on those aspects of popular politics characterised by a remarkable continuity in terms of language and ideas. As for my use of 'England' as opposed to Britain, this is a recognition of the fact that British history is the story of four nations. Much of what I have to say is relevant to the non-English parts of the United Kingdom. However, I have inserted the name 'England' in the title mainly for reasons of accuracy. This book is essentially about English politics but I also recognise that the term 'English history' conceals a diversity of regional (and other) experiences. Moreover, it should be said that many of the ideas and feelings presented here were not peculiar to England. Radicalism was very much the product of an Anglo-American dialogue in the later eighteenth century and there were comparable developments in Europe. It should also not be forgotten that Britain had a large empire which meant that political ideas always had a wider context.

More troubling perhaps is the definition of 'politics' which I take to mean the ways in which the distribution of power within society is understood and debated. This involves formal politics (such as electioneering and organisations such as political parties) but it also includes the less formal world of popular culture. This study is written in the belief that the common people have an intellectual history every bit as rich and important as the elite thinkers normally scrutinised by academics.

The study is organised as follows. Chapters One and Two introduce readers to the historical orthodoxies concerning nineteenth-century popular politics as they had developed by about 1980 (what I call the 'old analysis') and discuss the ways in which these orthodoxies have been challenged since then. Chapters Three and Four consider the new 'polity-centred' explanations for popular politics which require attention be paid not only to class but also to the nature of the state, the franchise and party formation as determinants of political culture. Chapters Five and Six explore the ideology of popular radicalism and consider alternatives to explanations based on class consciousness. Chapters Seven and Eight go into detail on one such alternative, national consciousness, and examine something often ignored by historians, popular conservatism. The Conclusion suggests ways in which the debate might be taken forward. Throughout, I am concerned to introduce readers to the texture and practice of popular political culture and to show what the field looks like after a period of vigorous revisionism. The traditional agenda of scholars in this field is now out of date and the arguments of many revisionists must be taken seriously. However, the old agenda is not altogether irrelevant and contains many perspectives lacking in recent writing. This study is intended to address the interpretive gap and for that reason I dub my approach 'post-revisionist'. This is very much a book about historiography, examining the ways in which historians construct their explanations. In this spirit, the book commences with a case study of the Queen Caroline affair that reveals the changing pattern of historical interpretation.

As we move away from the world of the Victorians, it may appear that their conflicts and achievements are no longer relevant in our global village with its information superhighway. This book is, however, written in the belief that the political arguments of the last century, the struggles that were won and (often) lost, the debates on democracy and the question of where power was to reside in society, remain as relevant in these days as they ever did.

Part I

The old analysis

1   Reinterpreting the Queen Caroline case

In 1820 Britain was rocked by one of the most bizarre episodes in its political history. This was the year that saw the death of George III. A far cry from the tyrannical despot that he had appeared in the early years of his reign, the king was considered by many to be the father of his people, a benevolent farmer who resembled the national emblem of John Bull. As the king withdrew from public life with old age and 'madness' (or rather, porphyria), his popularity had increased. By contrast, the new king was remarkably unpopular. The Prince Regent was reckoned by many to be a libertine whose lechery rendered him unfit to lead the nation. Exception was taken to his treatment of his wife, Caroline of Brunswick. The pair had married in 1795 mainly to persuade Parliament of the new-found respectability of the bankrupt Prince whose debts required payment. Their marriage was a disaster. Neither could abide the other and rumour had it that they spent only their wedding night together after which they went their separate ways. Caroline moved to the Continent in 1814 where it was believed she took an Italian lover, Bartolomeo Bergami, and, on one occasion, visited the brothel of the Dey of Tunis. In 1820, the new king, George IV, attempted to prevent her becoming queen.

Radical opinion was infuriated by his decision. Sympathy for Caroline had existed as early as 1796 when there were reports of their separation. In 1813, the agitator William Cobbett had taken up her cause when the Prince attempted to stop her seeing their daughter. With the coronation imminent, Caroline insisted on her right to be crowned queen. Alderman Matthew Wood, Whig MP for the City of London and a leading champion of Caroline, travelled to the Continent and persuaded her to return home. At Dover she received an enthusiastic reception from the crowd. Negotiations with Lord Liverpool's government to arrange a settlement broke down and George then demanded that she be put on trial for adultery through a

Bill of Pains and Penalties. Not only radicals but the public generally came to Caroline's rescue. Pamphlets, petitions and demonstrations on her behalf spread through the country. In Parliament, the Whig MP, Henry Brougham, who was acting as Caroline's attorney, flamboyantly contested the Government's case against the queen. Caroline became Britannia – the embodiment of the nation. Her lost rights became the people's lost rights. She replied to an address from supporters in St Pancras by saying that ' . . . those who degrade the queen have never manifested any repugnance in abridging the liberties of the people'.[1] This agitation was rooted in the concern that the monarchy apparently considered itself above the law, George IV having previously entered into an illegal marriage with Mrs Fitzherbert.[2] Although the ideology of the cause never amounted to much more than the struggle of 'Us' against 'Them', the Caroline movement dramatised the reality of 'Old Corruption', government by clique and cabal. Furthermore, it provided the means by which radicals suffering from a deluge of repressive legislation could agitate whilst appearing loyal to the state through their support for the queen. Although the Bill passed through the Lords, the government decided not to continue with it, a move that signalled a triumph for Caroline. She attended a ceremony of thanksgiving at St Paul's Cathedral and public meetings throughout Britain to celebrate her victory. The windows of unpopular government ministers were broken. Church bells were rung in support of the queen's victory and there was fury when any member of the clergy refused supporters access to the belfry of the local church. Many authorities banned firework demonstrations and swore in additional constables to keep the peace.[3] Given the government clampdown on popular political activity at that time, it was a spectacular mass mobilisation of opinion.

Having become a popular heroine, Caroline then lost favour by accepting a pension from the government. When the coronation took place, she attempted to gain admittance to Westminster Abbey in order to be crowned queen but was refused entry. She even had to endure the embarrassment of trying to enter by the back of the Abbey. Although crowds gathered to support her, there were no real disturbances. Nevertheless, when she died shortly afterwards, radicals frustrated government plans to quietly dispatch her body to Brunswick. A crowd intercepted the funeral procession and insisted that it should not exit through north London but instead pass through the city. The immense demonstration on her behalf led to violence and forced the resignation of the chief magistrate of Bow Street. It was the final moment of triumph both for Caroline and for Regency radicalism.

In his classic book, *The Making of the English Working Class* (1963), E.P. Thompson dismissed the Queen Caroline affair and devoted barely a page to it: 'Into the humbug of the Queen's case we need not inquire'.[4] In his view, the agitation revealed the failure of the revolutionary tradition that he was tracing. With its middle-class leadership and sympathy for an aristocrat, the movement did not fit into any pre-existing model of class development. Lacking any real political content, it was an embarrassment in the history of radicalism. Yet in recent years the Caroline affair has been reassessed with a flood of articles and books that provide an indication of the way in which historical practice has changed. Whereas social historians were formerly mainly interested in class, the recent literature on Queen Caroline reveals a whole set of new categories through which to interpret popular movements: gender, patriotism, ethnicity, populism, respectability, the public sphere and melodrama. The historiography of the Queen Caroline case is typical of the new ways in which popular politics is being analysed. Indeed the affair has come into its own as a key moment in political development. Layer upon layer of new meanings have come to light. Recent historians have not been concerned with the problem of 'authentic' class responses (which made the Caroline affair difficult to understand) but have analysed instead the evidence that exists on its own terms.

How has the case been reinterpreted? It is now clear that the agitation was distinctive for its role in presenting a relatively new figure in politics: Public Opinion. The cause created communities of moral outrage although 'public opinion' was mostly used at that time to refer to middle-class males.[5] In this new public sphere, the behaviour of the elite was open to criticism by all. Leonore Davidoff and Catherine Hall interpret the movement as a defining moment in the making of the English middle class. Rejecting the lax morality of the aristocracy, middle-class support for Caroline represented an assertion of its own values based on separate spheres (the division of civil society into public and private). The monarch's contempt for domesticity (his duty towards his wife) contrasted with the earnest respectability invested by the bourgeoisie in the home.[6] In retrospect, the Caroline case can be seen as part of a middle-class search for a monarchy that would deliver solid family values, a quest that concluded with the accession of Queen Victoria in 1837.

Nevertheless, the rhetoric of the movement appeared to be all inclusive, pitting the whole nation against the corrupt elite. The cause derived a great deal of support from artisan radicals such as the Thames shipwright John Gast. Whereas some radicals like Francis Place wished to simply discredit the monarchy, Gast admired the courage of the queen and agitated on her behalf. The movement served to re-establish political campaigning at a time when repressive government legislation (the Six Acts) threatened the possibility of any future radical action. I.J. Prothero argues that the simple existence of the agitation may have been more important than any political content it possessed.[7] Beyond formal politics, the cause was notable for the way in which it was taken up in the rough culture of common labourers; hence the fears for public order registered by magistrates and church-wardens throughout the country and particularly in the countryside where authorities had to deal with the anger of the mob whose carnival-like spirit manifested the continuity of eighteenth-century patterns of protest. This was also true of the ideology of the movement which, although hardly sophisticated, was not devoid of content. Supporters claimed that they were defending the constitution as established by the signing of Magna Charta by King John. In William Hone's pro-Caroline pamphlet entitled *The Queen and Magna Charta; Or, the Thing that John signed*, which went through at least five editions in 1820, Magna Charta was represented surrounded by the laws of England, the revolutionary Cap of Liberty, a lion with a crown and a dog with a collar labelled 'John Bull':

This is
THE STANDARD,
the
RALLYING SIGN,
round which
every
BRITON of HONOR
will join
To restore to their Country
their King and their Queen,
The blessings that Faction
would dare contravene,
And with heart and with hand
in a moment expel,
THE TRAITORS TO ENGLAND,
the offspring of Hell.
THE HORRIBLE VERMIN
the **RATS AND THE LEECHES**

> *Whom the Blood and the Treasure*
> *of Britain enriches.*
> *Whose pestilent breath*
> *if prolong'd, would consume*
> *The fruits of our country,*
> *Its verdure, and bloom.*
> *Destroy MAGNA CHARTA,*
> *and then in its place*
> *Allow us like slaves,*
> *to exist in disgrace.*[8]

This squib captures the essence of popular political thought: its belief in a benevolent constitution under threat, its opposition to self-interest, its fear of despotism and love of liberty, its heroic cadences and abiding patriotism.

Supporters and opponents of Queen Caroline expressed their views in terms of the nation. The iconography of crown and constitution suffused the movement. The above pamphlet depicted an Englishman, an Irishman and a Scotsman under their common (and relatively new) identity as Britons supporting Caroline's crown.[9] National identity was a crucial component of the movement, with the queen representing the people. This was assisted by the role of foreigners in the case who unwittingly helped define the Britishness of the queen's cause. Her former servant, Majocci, who testified against her, became a popular villain. His constant refrain during the trial, 'non mi riccordo' (I don't remember), became the subject of popular derision and he was actually burnt in effigy and attacked by the crowd. Xenophobia ran deep within the common people, with the foreigner providing an example of 'the other' against which national identity could be constructed.

Caroline drew support not only because of her constitutional status as queen but also because of her gender. Her cause has enjoyed renewed attention on account of the unprecedented participation of women. As Thomas Laqueur reveals in what is probably the most influential recent assessment of the case, women predominated in the crowds. A female petition from Nottingham had 7,800 signatures, another from Bristol had 11,047, whilst London women produced petitions with 17,652 names.[10] *The Queen and Magna Charta* was dedicated to 'the Ladies of Great Britain' and its cover featured Britannia with a parchment on which was written: 'To assert the Rights of Man/To avenge the wrongs of woman'.[11] Moreover, it was the first of several agitations during the century in which women were to represent themselves as defenders of communal morality. Such movements gave women a voice in a way that traditional radicalism based on artisan skill did not. The cause provided an opportunity to attack the double standard of sexual morality whereby men were allowed to exercise their sexuality outside marriage whilst women were expected to remain chaste. George IV, who had previously tried to prevent Caroline from seeing their daughter, was perceived as an enemy of the family and a debauched libertine. Anna Clark has drawn attention to the way in which plebeian women identified with Caroline as a victimised wife. The presence of a vigorous female lobby meant that male radicals were forced to incorporate women's demands in their political agenda.[12] The symbolism of the queen's plight therefore expanded the range of popular politics beyond the question of the constitution. Similarly, male radicals supported Caroline because of their increasing opposition to libertinism and because of their desire to defend the family.[13] Masculine support was usually enunciated in the language of chivalry. At a pro-Caroline demonstration in Alford, Lincolnshire, a man rode on horseback in front of a procession waving a sword as Caroline's champion and challenging anyone who would dispute her succession. The procession of London brassfounders to celebrate the queen's victory in January 1821 actually included eight knights on horseback in full armour.[14] The women of Nottingham asked 'all in whom the spirit of the days of chivalry are not utterly extinct' to support the queen.[15] Craig Calhoun argues that the Caroline agitation was a form of populism designed to preserve a traditional, community-based way of life.[16]

It should be clear by now that, as Laqueur suggests, the case was presented to the public through the lens of melodrama. Caroline was the wronged woman whilst George IV was an aristocratic seducer, both types familiar from the stage. For Laqueur, this ultimately trivialised the movement and rendered its political content redundant, explaining its failure. Anna Clark, by contrast, argues that it was melodrama that actually gave the movement its power and enabled it to reach a wider audience.[17] The melodrama of the queen's fate took no account of her actual behaviour with Bergami and others but this issue surfaced in the close cousin of melodrama, pornography. Anti-Caroline propagandists employed lewd images of the queen's immoral life on the Continent, but the majority of pornographic material assaulted George IV whose libertinism made him the target of bawdy prints. Iain McCalman sees the Caroline case as a highpoint of obscene populism where the underground press employed pornography to satirise and deflate its government opponents. Radical publishers such as William Benbow produced 'pro-Queen smut'.[18] The

Caroline case was therefore extremely complex. On the one hand, it embodied a deep respectability that was to be crucial not just to the middle class but also to many working-class politicians. On the other, it co-existed with what McCalman calls 'unrespectable radicalism'. Political identities contain a great deal of ambiguity. They are expressed through performance and role play. Emotions and feelings about the social order are as important as well thought-out political programmes. What we learn from the Queen Caroline affair is that politics is frequently about states of mind.

At the end of the day, the Caroline agitation was stopped in its tracks by the strength of the conservative counterblast which attacked the queen's morality and affirmed its loyalty to British institutions.[19] Popular conservatism was therefore as significant as radicalism. At an elite level, the affair also had some importance. It brought the Liverpool government into further disrepute and enabled the Whig opposition to define itself as a grouping uniquely sympathetic to 'public opinion'. Although not to enter government for another ten years, this sensitivity to public opinion was to prove a key to the Whig renaissance of the 1830s.

In the literature on the Queen Caroline case we can therefore find a range of readings that encapsulate the new agenda of historians of popular politics and which were not available in the 1960s. There is a new sensitivity to neglected groups such as women, to politics that were supposedly eccentric and non-class-specific. The new literature bears the imprint of developments in cultural history and current gender politics. The social and intellectual currents that enable historians to devise new explanations are the concern of this book.

2 From the old analysis to the new

After the Second World War, the politics of the people in the nineteenth century became a major historical industry. In part, this reflected the growth of interest in all matters Victorian that characterised the post-war period, but the reasons for it go deeper than that. From the late 1950s to the late 1970s a body of work was produced in social history that I call here the 'old analysis'. This is purely a convenient label for a diverse literature that was characterised by intense debate and disagreement. It drew on a variety of disciplines from sociology to anthropology and expanded the range of questions that historians asked and the sources they consulted. Subject material ranged from records of riots and strikes to the role of cartoons and popular song. Its sophistication (particularly in the work of historians like E.P. Thompson or Asa Briggs) meant that it was followed and emulated by scholars all over the world. Some of the scholars crudely lumped together here had little to say to each other. The 'old analysis' does not denote a school of thought so much as a body of work produced at a particular time. It was a matrix with different approaches to similar areas. If we are to understand what is distinctive about the post-1980 literature on the subject, we must comprehend something of the pioneering spirit that produced the old analysis. As will become clear, modern historians have been sitting on giants' shoulders.

THE ROOTS OF THE OLD ANALYSIS

Appropriately, the reasons for historical interest in popular politics tended to be political. Some historians were drawn to the subject because of a concern with democracy or the development of the constitution as part of the story of how Westminster government emerged. This interest had its roots in the school of thought which saw

British history as the inevitable unfolding of progress (what is known as the Whig interpretation of history). To be British was to enjoy a heritage of liberty. The nineteenth century provided the story of how, in a succession of Reform Acts, the British came to enjoy democracy. Other historians were attracted to the subject through a concern with social class and the emergence of a class society. Popular politics was perceived as a reflection of the growth of working-class consciousness. For Marxists, this was important because the proletariat was defined as the key vehicle of social and political transformation. On all sides, the past was a political weapon.

Before 1945, interest in popular politics had manifested itself in three different ways. First, it was covered by political history and the embryonic discipline of political science. Starting with Henry Jephson's *The Platform* in 1892, a succession of works demonstrated how the people became a presence in politics and how the modern party system emerged.[1] Amongst these were several historians of the Chartist movement, the most important of whom – the Fabian Mark Hovell – saw Chartism in terms of the coming of democracy.[2] His focus on the essentially political nature of Chartism anticipated many revisionist themes discussed later in this chapter.

Second, the study of popular politics had its roots in labour history, particularly the study of working-class institutions inaugurated by the Fabians Sidney and Beatrice Webb with their *History of Trade Unionism* (1894). The Webbs' most important successor was the socialist G.D.H. Cole who developed the field of labour history almost single handed. His books set out the basis for 'the forward march of labour' thesis which underpinned the old analysis.[3] The labour movement was shown to have risen on the back of industrial capitalism. Cole was mainly concerned with trade unions but his work went beyond this. For example, *Chartist Portraits* (1941) was a major examination of radical leadership in the early Victorian period.

Finally, the study of popular politics was developed by the very new discipline of social history. Here, the most important work before the Second World War was by the advanced Liberals J.L. and Barbara Hammond and their books about the working class during the early Industrial Revolution, particularly *The Village Labourer* (1911) and *The Age of the Chartists, 1832–1854* (1930). They discussed the ways in which society was remodelled in the industrial period and the working class brutalised. The modern literature on patterns of popular protest is ultimately derived from them.

Important as this work was, it was treated as marginal within the larger historical discipline which continued to emphasise high politics.

As late as 1945, it was still assumed that the history of the working class and its politics could not be written, either because the subject was unimportant or the sources did not exist. This changed dramatically in the post-war period for several reasons. First, there was the expansion of higher education in Britain and the professionalisation of the discipline which intensified study. Second, there was the election of Clement Attlee's Labour government in 1945 and the (apparent) victory of socialism with the coming of the welfare state. The 'forward march of labour' therefore had practical relevance. Finally, there was the massive growth of social history which began to colonise the subject. In this pioneering moment, an approach emerged that stressed the rise of class society and the politicisation of the common people, the approach here termed the old analysis. Although the subject of intense debate, most historians would recognise the outlines of the following narrative.

THE OLD ANALYSIS

Popular politics in the nineteenth century was understood in terms of a series of key caesuras or moments of change. The old analysis neatly compartmentalised the century and assumed a discontinuity in popular politics that had not been the case in the work of earlier historians like Simon Maccoby. The great theme of popular politics was the growth of class consciousness both in the middle and working classes.

Historians usually saw the emergence of popular politics as beginning with John Wilkes' career as a popular demagogue in the 1760s, attacking George III and espousing a wider franchise. His adoption by the mob ('Wilkes and Liberty') revealed a growing understanding of politics among the common people. Agitators such as Major Cartwright and Christopher Wyvill took up the cause of Reform (meaning the expansion of the franchise) in the 1770s. The American Revolution with its demand for 'No Taxation Without Representation' had a considerable impact in Britain, but what really transformed popular politics was what Eric Hobsbawm called the 'dual revolution': the coincidence of the French Revolution and the Industrial Revolution.[4] Support for events in France led to demands that the revolution should be imported. Thomas Paine's *Rights of Man* (1791–2) expressed these sentiments and established the basic framework of radicalism. A revolutionary movement emerged in the 1790s although it was driven underground by a programme of state repression. At the same time, the Industrial Revolution transformed society and the landscape. Over a fifty-year period, a factory proletariat emerged that could potentially respond to a politics based on class.

Indeed the actual language of 'class' entered the English vocabulary in the later eighteenth century. The stresses of the new factory system threatened traditional artisans such as handloom weavers. Their distress was evident in the phenomenon of machine breaking known as Luddism in 1811–12. Supporters of General Ludd (a fictional Robin Hood figure common in these forms of protest) destroyed steam-powered machinery particularly in Nottinghamshire and the West Riding of Yorkshire.

The end of the Napoleonic wars in 1815 represents the first key moment of change. The economic depression that followed brought social distress to the working classes that expressed itself in a short-lived revival of Luddism but, more importantly, in the revival of the mass platform, the embodiment of extra-parliamentary opinion through associations, newspapers, petitions and charismatic leaders. William Cobbett and Henry Hunt renewed the old call for political reform as a solution to the depression. Between 1815 and 1820, there was a dramatic upsurge of radical activity that climaxed in the Peterloo massacre in 1819. The spectacle of 'Orator' Henry Hunt addressing a crowd at St Peter's Field in Manchester led the local magistrate to call in the yeomanry to disperse the meeting. The carnage that resulted included eleven deaths and hundreds of wounded civilians. In the wake of the uproar that followed, Lord Liverpool's government enacted legislation clamping down on radicalism, a move made all the more pressing by the Cato Street conspiracy, an attempt to assassinate the cabinet. This was the background to the Queen Caroline affair.

The first third of the nineteenth century therefore witnessed the making of the working class and specifically a working-class political movement that E.P. Thompson controversially claimed was the most significant presence in political life during the struggle that led up to the Great Reform Act of 1832. The Act that essentially enfranchised the middle class (another class that had been made during the industrial period) marked a caesura. Working-class disappointment at not gaining the vote then conditioned the politics of the next two decades. Prior to 1832, the most obvious alliance had been a union of the middle and working classes against the aristocracy that dominated power. The Act of 1832, however, created a new ruling class based on the upper and middle classes against the rest. The next two decades proved particularly turbulent because of the social problems caused by the Industrial Revolution: bad housing and sanitation, overcrowding, exploitation in the workplace (particularly in the form of long working days). This then generated a series of agitations such as the movement against the Poor Law Amendment Act of 1834 and the Factory Movement to reduce the working day and remove female and child labour from the workplace. These movements climaxed in Chartism.

The Chartists have enjoyed a central position in the historiography of the nineteenth century not only because they represented the largest popular mobilisation of the century but also because they were held by some historians to represent a new politics of class consciousness. Chartism was the result of the economic distress of the working class even though the six points of the People's Charter (universal manhood suffrage, annual parliaments, the secret ballot, the payment of MPs, the abolition of the property qualification for MPs and equal electoral districts) were all political demands. As G.D.H. Cole put it: 'The Chartist movement was essentially an economic movement with a purely political programme'.[5] It represented a new stage in popular politics, rejecting industrial society. The defeat of the third and final Chartist petition in 1848 marked another major break in the history of popular politics.

A new period began after 1848 that lasted up to the mid-1880s. Based on a spirit of compromise that replaced class hostility, it was backed up by improvements in the economy and a rise in living standards throughout the 1850s and 1860s and was symbolised by the popularity of the Great Exhibition of 1851. Popular politics was dominated by the artisans (or 'labour aristocracy') who abandoned the extreme radicalism of the early Victorian period in favour of class collaboration. An ideology which, for historians such as John Foster (see pp. 24–5), had been proto-revolutionary, was replaced by reformism.[6] So complete was the change that the more prosperous parts of the urban working class were given the vote in 1867. Moreover, the trade union leadership succeeded in lobbying Gladstone's government for legal recognition of trade unionism with the labour laws of 1871. The class-based radicalism of the Chartists was a thing of the past. Where workers once read Tom Paine, they now read Samuel Smiles, who advocated hard work and self improvement as the solution to poverty. With some notable exceptions, the popular politics of this period was relatively unexplored.

However, this spirit of compromise (or 'equipoise') was shattered by the experiences of the 1880s. The problems of poverty reasserted themselves with concern over 'Outcast London' and other major cities. The word 'unemployment' entered the English vocabulary for the first time. The strict divisions between skilled and unskilled that had characterised the working classes up to that point became increasingly blurred with the advent of deskilling. With the success of the matchgirls' strike at Bryant and May in 1888 and the London dock strike of 1889, unskilled workers began to unionise. The last two decades of the century therefore represent a coherent period when a more homogeneous working class emerged. Significantly, this was also a period when the ideology of socialism was revived in a revolutionary form by the Social Democratic Federation (SDF) in 1884 and in a reformist shape by the Fabian Society the same year. The rise of labour was therefore accompanied by an ideology that could make sense of a mature class society. The Independent Labour Party (ILP), formed in Bradford in 1893, gave voice to this new class militancy. In 1900, the Labour Representation Committee (LRC) was formed, based on the ILP, the SDF, the Fabians and the trade unions. This was the formal beginning of the Labour Party which would eventually oust the Liberals as the chief progressive party and the party of the working class (although only after the disastrous split in the Liberals during the First World War). From the 1870s, the Conservative Party had increasingly gained the support of the middle classes. Therefore, by 1918, the two-party system mirrored the class system. Without a secure class base, the Liberals were doomed.

This narrative has obviously ignored much and most of its details were heavily debated throughout the 1960s and 1970s. However, the broad outline with its distinctive breaks in 1832, 1848 and the mid-1880s constituted the core of the old analysis. There was a general belief in social explanations for politics. The growth of the study of working-class life carried with it the assumption that social developments fed into the politics of the working class. We now need to consider the strengths and weaknesses of the old analysis in order to establish what is distinctive about the new revisionism.

DEBATING POPULAR POLITICS

In the 1960s, social history was in the ascendant and the history of popular politics was nurtured under its aegis. This was the basis of the old analysis. The upsurge of interest was in part the responsibility of the Communist Party Historians' Group in the 1950s. Its membership included E.P. Thompson, Eric Hobsbawm, George Rudé and Christopher Hill, whose work on the English revolution of the seventeenth century proved a deep influence, as did that of their mentor, Dona Torr.[7] The younger generation included Raphael Samuel, later co-founder of the History Workshop movement, whose purpose was to excavate the history of everyday life. Unashamedly partisan, the Group opened up the history of the working class and created a new approach that became known as 'history from below'. Outside the Group, the old analysis had its basis in a democratic, vaguely leftist concern to produce a people's history, something that was needed despite the erosions of class society in Harold Macmillan's England with its mass consumerism. Many of its practitioners had a background in adult and workers' education. The impetus for this new social history was derived from the fact that the majority of the population, and certainly the working class, had been excluded from history as it was then written. Social historians had to find ways of providing those who had been silenced with a voice. This was achieved using a variety of methods. The papers of the radical Francis Place were ransacked for their elaborate documentation of early nineteenth-century popular politics, as were radical newspapers such as the Chartist *Northern Star*. Records of crime and disturbance were studied as ways of entering popular culture. For example, some of the most useful sources for Chartism are the Home Office prison records on Chartist prisoners. The crowd was retrieved as a major historical actor and defended against claims of irrationality. Some forms of riot were interpreted as social protest. The best examples of this are E.P. Thompson's work on the eighteenth-century moral economy and Hobsbawm and Rudé's study of the Captain Swing disturbances in 1830.[8] Popular agitations were examined, hence the concern with Chartism. A huge literature of working-class autobiography was discovered and in many cases re-published. This literature tended to privilege the literate artisan classes. Autobiographies by these rather untypical members of the working class were intended for public consumption as elaborate pieces of self justification.

The most influential book produced by the Communist Party Historians' Group was E.P. Thompson's *The Making of the English Working Class* (1963) which traced the emergence of a working-class movement during the early Industrial Revolution. Thompson left the Communist Party in 1956 in protest at the Soviet invasion of Hungary, a move that also signalled his break with orthodox Marxism. His book detailed the Jacobin political inheritance amongst artisans, particularly in the revolutionary underground of the 1790s which adopted Paine's *Rights of Man* and was responsible for 'planting the Liberty Tree'. Making no concessions to academic proprieties concerning detachment, Thompson spoke for the losers, the marginalised and the neglected, whom he promised to rescue from 'the enormous condescension of posterity'. He defended the Luddites, seeing them not as enemies of modernity but as poor people struggling for their livelihoods and engaged in primitive forms of collective bargaining. He sought out 'obsolete' handloom weavers and farm labourers dispossessed by enclosure. Taking up the story of Parliamentary Reform after 1815, he revealed how a working-class movement had come into being such that by 1830 Britain was close to revolution. His crucial insight in this angry, defiant book was that politics was an essential part of the lives of the common people which informed all of their experience. For him, class was not an objective thing that existed unproblematically. Instead, class was inseparable from class consciousness. He emphasised the culture of class, something that was felt and experienced. This also meant that political traditions were important and complex. Unrest was about more than hunger, reflecting an increasingly mature understanding of social developments.

Much of the social history produced in the 1960s and 1970s employed a soft Marxist framework and was heavily influenced by Thompson's discussion of class in the preface to *The Making*. What was attractive about Thompson's approach was that his interpretation provided the working class with agency. It was depicted as active, taking part in its own making and not just as the passive receptacle of power from above. Classes were treated as historical phenomena that could be made and unmade. Moreover, Thompson noted that it was impossible to find a 'pure specimen of class'. Instead, he argued that:

> The class experience is largely determined by the productive relations into which men are born – or enter involuntarily. Class-consciousness is the way in which these experiences are handled in cultural terms: embodied in traditions, value-systems, ideas, and institutional forms. If the experience appears as determined, class-consciousness does not.[9]

This interpretation was sophisticated and grappled with the complexity of experience rather than reducing it to the dictates of a pre-determined theory.

Non-Marxist historians (although usually on the left) came to conclusions that were not very different. The Society for the Study of Labour History (founded in 1960) investigated the way in which trade unions and the labour movement became a presence in British society. Asa Briggs and the contributors to his *Chartist Studies* (1959) launched the modern wave of research into the movement. Their innovation was to argue that Chartism could only be fully appreciated through local studies. This not only highlighted the movement's diversity but was an attempt to record the activities of the rank and file. In the earlier generation, Cole's *Chartist Portraits* had only been concerned with leaders like Feargus O'Connor. In the same spirit,

J.F.C. Harrison's *Robert Owen and the Owenites in Britain and America* (1969) opened up the lives of the Owenite Socialists where previous studies of Owenism had been restricted to the life and writings of Owen alone. The importance of locality meant that urban politics were increasingly investigated. Derek Fraser and E.P. Hennock demonstrated that for most people, politics was a matter of what was happening nearby rather than at Westminster.[10]

For all its diversity, what united the old analysis was the importance of class and its relationship to politics. The exact form of this relationship was much debated. There were divisions over whether class led to class consciousness. This division even existed within Marxism. E.P. Thompson argued that a distinct working-class consciousness existed by 1830. Eric Hobsbawm rejected this, countering that class consciousness was fluid for most of the period under discussion and that it was only the maturity of the industrial capitalist economy that allowed for a fully-developed class consciousness in the last few decades of the century.[11] Similarly, J.F.C. Harrison pointed out that the language of class did not completely supersede other forms of social terminology in the first half of the century and that Owenites and radical millenarians ignored it. This did not rule out the existence of intense class conflict – especially during the Chartist years – or the role of radical movements in political education and the generation of class consciousness.[12]

During the heyday of the old analysis, work on popular politics was not the monopoly of social historians. Although political history was unfashionable, associated as it was with high politics, it developed new and exciting ways of dealing with the sources and became open to influences from other disciplines. Although distinct from the social history perpetuated by the old analysis, the two shared much. Political historians were inspired by the modern science of psephology (the study of elections). In Britain and America, elaborate forms of social science methodology were created for the investigation of electoral behaviour. The influence of David Butler at Nuffield College, Oxford was important. Amongst Butler's assistants who performed field work on elections in the 1950s were the future political historians H.J. Hanham and Kenneth O. Morgan.[13] Increasing attention was devoted to the emergence of modern party structure and the social forces that brought this about. Pollbook data was employed to uncover the sociology of elections. The coming of the secret ballot in 1872 may have been a great step forward for democracy but it was bad news for historians. Before that date, voting had been a public activity with the results often recorded in print (pollbooks), generating an immensely useful set of data that could be employed to trace the changing nature of the nineteenth-century electorate. Other new sources included local newspapers (which recorded electoral campaigns in each constituency in great detail), the private papers of politicians, parliamentary papers and Charles Dod's contemporary works of reference on the parliamentary system.[14] What emerged therefore amongst political historians was not simply more work on high politics but an attempt at a social analysis of politics.

For example, D.C. Moore presented a sociological interpretation of why the 1832 Reform Act made little difference to the parliamentary system and why the same kind of people were elected despite the widened franchise. His explanation rested on the role of deference which held the system together, particularly in rural areas.[15] For the mid-Victorian period, the political system was treated by H.J. Hanham's *Elections and Party Management* (1959), which detailed the growth of party organisation in the constituencies after 1867, and John Vincent's *The Formation of the British Liberal Party, 1857–68* (1966). Hanham and Vincent were both concerned with the development of a two-party system at a popular level and the way in which, as Hanham put it, 'the nation accustomed itself to the notion of democracy'.[16] The electoral sociology of late Victorian Britain was investigated by Henry Pelling who mapped out the distribution of seats in the wake of the 1884–5 Reform Acts and linked patterns of voting to social structure.[17] Political historians tended to see the relationship between politics and social class in complex ways. Peter Clarke suggested that Victorian politics was conditioned as much by status as by class. By status, he meant politics determined by cultural factors like religion or ethnicity rather than by simple material interests. It was only in the Edwardian period that politics came to be based mainly on class. However, the rise of class did not mean the automatic victory of the Labour Party. Clarke argued that the 'strange death of Liberal England' was not inevitable. The New Liberalism was able to withstand the rise of class politics and the Liberal Party was only destroyed by the split between Asquith and Lloyd George during the First World War.[18]

Returning to the old analysis, its strength was that it insisted on the importance of culture. By and large, social historians refused to reduce politics to crude economic determinism (although the economic was never left out). Instead, they focused on language, custom, ritual and belief structures. All of these played a role in determining the nature of politics. This was true even of some political historians (often accused of adopting a 'top down' approach in contrast to history from below).

For example, John Vincent's work on rank and file Liberalism was a painstaking account of what it meant to be a Liberal in the mid-Victorian period. What mattered for social historians was the category of experience, often studied with an anthropological approach. Religion (particularly Methodism), community and tradition were essential to popular political culture. Out of this came a concern with the flashpoints of protest: the strike, the riot, the threatening letter. The working class seemed anything but passive to social historians, especially those who adopted the pessimistic side in the controversy over whether standards of living rose or fell during the early Industrial Revolution.

This generated a subsidiary question: why was there no revolution in Britain (given the existence of appalling social conditions, an exploited labour force and the inspiration of revolution abroad from 1789 onwards)? This question informed the shape of much research in the 1970s. Answers to the problem varied. A great deal of attention was devoted to the role of social control by the upper and middle classes in the form of education or the application of the law.[19] E.P. Thompson pointed to the importance of constitutionalism in framing popular political thought. In his work on the eighteenth century, he argued that the law was not simply integral to ruling-class hegemony but that 'some part of it . . . was taken over as part of the rhetoric of the plebeian crowd, of the "free-born Englishman" with his inviolable privacy, his *habeas corpus*, his equality before the law'.[20] The continuing importance of these categories naturally modified the development of a revolutionary consciousness.

Another approach was posited by the labour aristocracy debate. The great problem facing social historians who focused on the rise of class consciousness in the early nineteenth century was how to explain what happened to the working-class movement created by the traumas of industrialisation that flourished in the form of Chartism. Inspired by Lenin, Eric Hobsbawm argued that skilled workers who had previously been in the vanguard of class-conscious agitations sold out in the post-Chartist years and became reformist, accepting the economic situation as it was and working for the best deal within it. The working class therefore lost its leadership and the possibility of a class-based challenge to capitalism foundered.[21] In the 1970s, this thesis produced a series of studies that examined the role of the labour aristocracy. John Foster's *Class Struggle and the Industrial Revolution* (1974) was the most debated. A Marxist study of Oldham and two other industrial towns, it pinpointed a critical shift at mid-century whereby the bourgeoisie managed to buy off and co-opt a key section of the labour movement. The labour aristocracy became key figures within a new system of discipline in the workplace and abandoned the revolutionary class consciousness which had characterised Oldham's politics in the 1830s and 1840s. Support for education and temperance served to produce the proletariat that the bourgeoisie wanted – orderly and disciplined. The labour aristocracy was central to the re-composition of capitalist authority. Foster's work was based on an austere form of economic determinism which was not shared by either his critics or the other historians who studied the labour aristocracy. In separate studies of Edinburgh and Kentish London, Robert Gray and Geoffrey Crossick focused on the way in which economic experiences were mediated by cultural and ideological factors.[22] They disputed the possibility that a bourgeois ideology could be simply imposed on the working class. The labour aristocracy was portrayed as more assertive, its social values determined not by middle-class indoctrination but by pre-existing working-class traditions of independence and craft pride. In political terms, this allowed for alliances with liberalism and assaults on local patrician elites but not demands for any substantial social change, a politics of status rather than of class.

The mid-Victorian compromise broke down in the mid-1880s, which proved to be a turning point for the labour movement with the development of independent working-class organisations, militancy and the new ideology of socialism. The key debate was over the relationship between the rise of Labour and the decline of Liberalism.[23] Although the roots and ideology of socialism were extensively traced and the events of the late nineteenth century seen as a distinctive stage in the forward march of labour, historians of the left were not always triumphalist. What emerged at the end of the century for some was not socialism so much as 'labourism', a specific form of political consciousness based on trade unions rather than class that was limited in its ambition for social change.[24]

The old analysis therefore painted a portrait of a heroic but slightly unsatisfactory labour movement. Some historians hoped their work would provide the working class with agency (a sense of its potential and ability to shape its own destiny). For example, History Workshop became the vehicle in the 1970s for a politically engaged history from below that attempted to unite workers and historians. But in the 1980s, the forward march of labour was halted.

REVISIONISM

The old analysis was a series of attempts to view popular politics with a stress on class, culture and community. However, there were real problems with an account based on class and the 'forward march of labour' which explains why it began to come unstuck. First of all, the approach romanticised the working class which Marxist and labour historians believed would fulfil its destiny as the agent of historical change. Apathetic or non-political workers did not merit much discussion. In a review of *The Making of the English Working Class*, Geoffrey Best noted that there was very little on the 'flag-saluting, foreigner-hating, peer respecting side of the plebeian mind'.[25] The traditional narrative had assumed that there were such things as autonomous class cultures and a working-class ideology (represented by rather untypical groups of artisans). Too often, this ideology was assumed to be socialism, and popular politics became simply the story of how the working class came to discover socialism. Every political struggle was an anticipation of the socialist future. Those activists such as the Chartist Ernest Jones who actually became socialists were particularly prized. Our examination of the Queen Caroline affair revealed the complexity of popular beliefs that the old analysis failed to sufficiently address.

During the 1980s, the traditional narrative of popular politics came under repeated challenge. The background to this was the continued election of Conservative governments assisted by a considerable working-class vote. Deindustrialization and heavy unemployment transformed the nature of the post-war working class. The whole intellectual edifice of socialism and the left was undermined by the fall of the Berlin Wall in 1989 and the collapse of Soviet Communism. The claims of sociology but also of determinist forms of thought such as Marxism fell by the wayside. Social explanations involving profound economic forces and class were abandoned in favour of a new focus on politics.[26] The revisionists of the Thatcher years often had little in common but collectively they undermined the premises of the traditional narrative. There was nothing unusual about the history of popular politics. During the same period, topics like the English Revolution and the French Revolution underwent fierce revisionist scrutiny.[27] What was peculiar to the subject was that most (but not all) of the revisionists were on the left. There were five areas in which the old analysis was challenged.

First, the premises of the traditional narrative which stressed the role of the Industrial Revolution were undermined by the new economic history. New data on industrial development in the early nineteenth century suggested that economic 'take off' was not so great or quick as had previously been assumed. Indeed, some economic historians went so far as to doubt the existence of an Industrial Revolution.[28] Instead of an Industrial Revolution located in the years 1780–1830, increasing emphasis was placed upon a much more protracted period of industrialisation, lasting over a hundred years at the very least. Economic growth in the early nineteenth century was mainly restricted to cotton textiles, iron and steel. Most production took place in small workshops as late as the 1850s. This severely undermined the idea of a factory proletariat emerging sometime before 1830. Instead, historians began to talk about the 'long eighteenth century', demonstrating how the economy of the first half of the nineteenth century had more in common with the economy of the eighteenth rather than the twentieth century. In contrast to the view that it was an economic backwater disrupted by industrial take off, the eighteenth century was reclaimed as an enterprising commercial society. Taking the Industrial Revolution out of the picture disrupted traditional class explanations of popular politics although it did explain why, in a workshop-based economy, politics remained dominated by artisans. Whilst there was no intrinsic reason why this should have been the case, the demise of the Industrial Revolution signalled a departure from explanations based on economic determinism.

Second, the idea of the 'long eighteenth century' helped produce the most important revisionist attack on the traditional narrative. Gareth Stedman Jones' article 'Rethinking Chartism' challenged the older view that Chartism was a response to a new form of industrial class society (see Chapter Three).[29] Stedman Jones emphasised instead the 'relative autonomy of the political', arguing that political developments could not be read off from an a priori social perspective. The insights of political historians, once so unfashionable, came to be seen as more profound. Explanations based on social determinism, particularly of the Marxist variety, were thrown into question. Studies of eighteenth-century political culture revealed that popular involvement in politics went back further than previously thought, undermining the distinctiveness of the nineteenth century.[30] Where the old analysis had been characterised by its emphasis on decisive breaks that shaped the course of popular politics, revisionists have emphasised the essential continuity of political language, ideas and culture from the eighteenth century onwards (see Chapter Five).

A third area of criticism came from the new women's historians who complained that the traditional narrative was essentially about male workers. Women were largely excluded from the account despite the fact that the archetypal proletarian in the nineteenth century was a woman. With the exception of the work of Sheila Rowbotham and Dorothy Thompson, women's considerable political activity had been ignored.[31] Hence Barbara Taylor's *Eve and the New Jerusalem* (1983), a study of women and Owenite Socialism, was a breakthrough. The coming of women's history, however, meant a new set of narratives. The separate spheres of public and private were understood to be as important a division as class. Gender was integral to class formation. Many of the working-class institutions celebrated by traditional labour history (such as trade unions) were re-interpreted as male dominated organisations. Jutta Schwarzkopf and Anna Clark demonstrated how gender and the maintenance of patriarchy were essential to the Chartists. Previously seen as heroic class warriors, Chartists were now shown to have been active in trying to keep women in the home. For Clark, artisans may have been part of an intellectual vanguard but they were also misogynists who excluded women from the workplace and beat their wives.[32] Chapter Six deals with the ways in which radicalism needs to be re-assessed in light of the insight that gender underpinned the whole network of social life.

The continued success of the Conservative Party in the 1980s led to a greater interest in popular conservatism, discussed in Chapter Eight. Previously, the chief object of study had been radicalism and socialism. Greater attention was given to the development of the Conservative Party and the culture that sustained it. In contrast to social history's emphasis on class conflict, there was a new sensitivity to consensus and the working class' incorporation into the new social and political system. The dramatic popularity of the Falklands expedition in 1982 put nationalism and xenophobia on the agenda. Whereas historians in the 1970s had downplayed the idea of a patriotic working class, a new history of patriotism investigated the extensive role of imperialism in working-class life.[33]

Finally, Patrick Joyce in *Visions of the People* (1991) and *Democratic Subjects* (1994) drew on the new tide of post-modernist and post-structuralist ideas to focus on non-class identities. He urged that the identities of 'the people', 'the nation' and of 'humanity' were at least as important in constructing mentalities as was class. Furthermore, post-structuralism undermined the whole premise of traditional social history.[34] Whilst most historians believe themselves to be re-creating a pre-existing reality, post-structuralists hold that 'reality' is simply a construction of language. The crux of Thompson's argument in *The Making of the English Working Class* was the importance of the category of 'experience'. Joan Wallach Scott, a leading advocate of post-structuralism, argued by contrast that 'experience' was a creation of historians, the 'social' being a construct of narrative.[35] These have so far proved to be minority positions within the historical profession. The main significance of this particular wave of revisionism is that, in contrast to the picture presented by the old analysis, it suggested that no single narrative of popular politics was possible. For revisionists, popular politics can only be understood through a maze of competing narratives that focus on the polity, the nation, gender and ideology. Therefore, not only was the traditional narrative of popular politics challenged but the whole agenda of history itself. Class-based social history appeared in danger of no longer being relevant.

It should be said that during the 1980s and 1990s there have been many high quality studies of popular politics that have continued to follow the Thompsonian agenda, particularly in the area of rural history. Ian Dyck, Alun Howkins and Roger Wells all revealed the importance of class in the development of radicalism.[36] Elsewhere, John Belchem and James Epstein actively confronted much of the new revisionism in their work to make better sense of class-based categories and employed many of the new insights.[37]

So where do we go from here? Whilst the traditional narrative has been rocked, Belchem and Epstein show that it has not been completely undermined. Clearly, the task of historians now is to produce a narrative that is richer, more complex and restores the things the traditional narrative silenced. These different kinds of revisionism have considerable implications for historical practice in the new century. The rest of this book will discuss how the task of writing the history of popular politics has changed and how it might develop.

Part II

New directions

3   The peculiarities of politics

In recent years, it has been common for historians to complain that social history has ignored politics.[1] Although popular politics was examined through the discipline of social history and many historians were themselves intensely political, nevertheless the realm of politics was deemed unproblematic. As we saw in Chapter Two, both Marxists and many non-Marxists believed that politics was a reflection of the economic base. This chapter will review the ways in which revisionist historians have rejected the premises of this approach and begun to rethink the relationship between politics and society. The characteristic of this new school of historians is their belief in the 'relative autonomy of the political'.

The essence of the revisionist case is that there is a gap between social structure and political ideology. The role of politics is to provide a language and set of ideas that help the individual make sense of society. For example, working people often do not become militant even when they are suffering hardship. They only agitate when a political language provides a diagnosis of the sources of their problem and establishes a viable strategy to deal with it. In other words, hunger by itself does not spur action; politics is necessary to provide the idea that hunger is not something to be endured. Furthermore, revisionists argue that the political has a dynamic and momentum of its own (determined partly by the nature of the state). As we shall see, radicals in early industrial England often diagnosed problems in terms of corrupt state power rather than through the language of class. They claimed to be protesting on behalf of the English constitution. Popular politics usually adopted this constitutionalist form. We therefore have to take both ideology and the political framework seriously. This will be called here a 'polity-centred' reading where change happens through new events and configurations in politics rather than through developments in the economy. It is the political that gives meaning to social and economic phenomena, determining the timing, form and language of popular politics. This chapter explores the contours of this approach as well as its strengths and weaknesses. Revisionists are often unclear about the value of social and economic history (at least for interpreting politics). I will argue that rather than negating 'society-centred' explanations, we have the makings of a new, more complex form of social history.

THE RELATIVE AUTONOMY OF THE POLITICAL

The intellectual roots of revisionism can be found in a variety of disciplines in the 1960s and 1970s. Within history, paradoxically, the work of E.P. Thompson was fundamental. Although his account of popular politics in *The Making of the English Working Class* was the centrepiece of the old analysis, Thompson eschewed economic reductionism and viewed the state and political forms in a sophisticated way. His work showed that although the mode of production was important, the link between the social and the political was not precise and that 'consciousness' was an important part of working-class formation (something that cannot be simply inferred from the economic base because of the mediating role of culture). Writing in the Thompsonian vein, I.J. Prothero developed this by revealing how the political context was integral to the development of radical movements. The upsurge of radicalism in 1830 was normally held to be the product of the social and economic distress of that year (unemployment, poor wages, high wheat prices). However, Prothero argued that the distress of 1826 had been much worse but had not produced radicalism. The difference between 1826 and 1830 lay in the political context of the breakdown of the Wellington administration and the coming of Catholic Emancipation which introduced a fluidity in politics allowing radical arguments to be made openly and to carry conviction.[2] The 'relative autonomy of the political' was also evident in the early work of John Vincent who argued that 'class, not in the Marxian sense of economic class, nor in the colloquial sense of stratum, but class in the sense of a group contending over the structure of political authority, was the general ground of popular political orientation'.[3] For Vincent, it was debates within politics that generated class. The 'working class' was a political rather than economic category.

Another tributary from which the 'relative autonomy' draws is the resurgence of interest across the humanities in language (usually referred to as the 'linguistic turn'). It has been argued that knowledge is inseparable from the language in which it is couched. Language was integral to the new intellectual history associated with J.G.A. Pocock and Quentin Skinner; each paid attention to the context within which works of political thought were produced and, especially, the role of language in setting limits on how people think. In a different vein, post-structuralist literary critics argued that language constructs reality rather than the other way round. These trends established new ways of looking at political texts that had previously been read simply as products of social and economic experience. Language, it was suggested, had its own autonomy. Changes in historical circumstances were not always accompanied by changes in language although traditional forms of language could acquire new meanings in different historical circumstances.[4] We will explore this in Chapter Five with reference to the language of constitutionalism.

Not only was language re-thought but so also was the role of the state. Marxists had previously assumed that the state was the instrument of the ruling class. Marx and Engels wrote in *The Manifesto of the Communist Party* (1848) that 'the executive of the modern State is but a committee for managing the common affairs of the whole bourgeoisie'.[5] Yet Marx in *The Eighteenth Brumaire of Louis Bonaparte* (1852) also recognised that the state was an institution in its own right, separate from the rest of society, with its own bureaucracy and momentum. Modern Marxists have used this insight to debate what they see as the 'relative autonomy of the state', noting that in order to serve the interests of the ruling class, the state has to be independent of it so that it can mediate between different parts of the bourgeoisie.[6] The insight that the state could be autonomous and not simply the reflection of the economic base of society was taken up by sociologists who argue that 'it is fruitful to assume *both* that states are potentially autonomous and, conversely, that socioeconomic relations influence and limit state structures and activities'.[7] Whilst the state is not invariably autonomous, it plays a key role in determining the nature of politics.

The debate on the autonomy of the state contributed to the intellectual background behind Gareth Stedman Jones' article 'Rethinking Chartism' in his 1983 collection, *Languages of Class*.[8] His *Outcast London* (1971) had been one of the key Marxist histories of the 1970s which made his subsequent work more surprising. Stedman Jones was part of a wider intellectual current that sought to re-integrate the political back into the social, evident particularly in French history.[9] His new work marked a break with the post-war historiography that interpreted Chartism as a paradigm of class development, the first modern independent working-class movement. The early Victorian years were usually taken to represent a new stage in the capitalist

economy, triggering a social movement that expressed worker alienation under the industrial regime and anticipated future socialist
struggles. However, Stedman Jones asked why, if Chartism simply
expressed the new working-class consciousness, the six points of the
People's Charter were all political. Where previous scholars had
assumed that Chartist language was a code for class tensions, Stedman
Jones argued that the six points and hence political language had to be
taken at face value. Rejecting the traditional Marxist view of class, he
insisted that social and economic grievances could not account for
Chartism's constitutionalist form. In his view, the movement did not
reflect a new stage in economic development (a point confirmed by the
new economic history discussed in Chapter Two). Instead, it indicated
the continuity of an older constitutionalist radicalism dating back to
the 1770s, an example of the 'long eighteenth century'.

The Chartists were not necessarily anti-capitalist either. Their arguments were premised on political exclusion, most notably the failure of
the working class to obtain the vote in 1832. Hence class was a political identity rather than an economic one. For Chartists, the tension in
society was not between the working class and the middle class (as
Marxist theory would have it) but between the workers and the idle. In
particular, the aristocracy was seen as a parasite on the labour of
others. It dominated the state through the patronage system and used
it to levy unfair taxes. Chartism could therefore never become the
ideology of a single class. The mental world of the Chartists was still
framed by the traditional radical denunciations of 'Old Corruption' or
what Cobbett called 'The Thing'. This explains Chartist failure; its
analysis could not cope with the increasing liberalisation of the state,
evident in Peel's tax reforms and the repeal of the Corn Laws in 1846
which proved that the state was not only fair but capable of change.
The Chartist argument was therefore redundant.

This path-breaking work was to prove immensely important for a
new generation of scholars who used the idea of the relative autonomy
of the political to rethink the entire historiography of nineteenth-
century popular politics.[10] Revisionists self-consciously explored the
potential of Stedman Jones' approach for understanding popular politics more broadly, detaching radicalism from its links to class struggle.
Popular liberalism was no longer seen as an example of the poverty of
mid-Victorian politics but as a rational attempt to establish a relationship between the state and the labour movement. Explanations based
on the labour aristocracy were discarded. In place of a narrative structured around discontinuities, such as the defeat of Chartism in 1848
and Labour's turning point in the 1880s, revisionists focused on the

continuity of radicalism (see Chapter Five). The relationship between the state and the political public was brought into question. Revisionists particularly focused on the way in which collective identities such as 'class' emerged. These identities were not seen as the inevitable product of industrial society but as interests forged in the context of political debate. Patrick Joyce expanded on Stedman Jones' work on language, exploring the culture of industrial England and drawing attention to non-class identities which he called 'populism'.[11] Much of this work would no doubt have happened without Stedman Jones. It was also extremely diverse both in subject matter and theoretical range. However, at least in Britain, Stedman Jones' contribution was pivotal in opening up the idea of the 'relative autonomy of the political'.

'Rethinking Chartism' was not in any way uncontroversial, generating an impressive series of extended replies from historians.[12] Although responses varied, many defended the importance of class in a conventional economic sense and insisted on the social nature of radicalism. Stedman Jones' application of the methods of intellectual history to plebeian movements was considered inappropriate. It was noted that there was no room in his account for working-class agency. His discussion of language was criticised for ignoring both gender and the multiplicity of meanings that were part of radical communication. Thus the idea that Chartism could never become the ideology of a specific class failed to take account of the way constitutionalist language could take class forms. Above all, Stedman Jones seemed to insist on a pure definition of class and class consciousness against which Chartism inevitably fell short.

The body of work thrown up by the idea of the 'relative autonomy of the political' has opened up new agendas. Historians have been forced to engage with the actual language of politics and the role of political strategies in constructing alliances between diverse groups of people. Non-class identities such as nationhood, religion and status politics have been taken seriously once more. Identity is no longer seen as fixed but multi-layered, as noted in the discussion of Queen Caroline in Chapter One. Overall, this perspective has banished reductionist interpretations of politics.

Rather than speak of autonomy (relative or otherwise), it might be better to think in terms of the peculiarities of politics. Popular politics was not just influenced by social and economic trends. Revisionism teaches us that its agenda was also determined by the nature of the polity. The construction of political strategies was complex because it involved turning groups of people with often various and competing concerns into popular movements such as Chartism. Thus, rather than negating social history, a polity-centred history actually enhances it, drawing our attention to the transformative power of politics. This aspect of the political process should be distinguished from the old Marxist idea of false consciousness which held that workers were frequently duped by capitalist ideology into accepting the status quo. For revisionists, political ideology, far from pulling the wool over the eyes of the proletariat, has an enabling function. They insist that ideas must be taken seriously. The adoption of radicalism and liberalism (as opposed to socialism) by workers was a rational decision, based on a realistic appraisal of the political situation. How might these new insights be applied?

4 A polity-centred history?

Rethinking the state, the franchise and party formation

The enduring impact of revisionism is likely to be the recognition that the political context is vital for understanding class. This chapter will explore three important determinants of political culture – the state, the franchise and party formation – in order to explain the framework within which ordinary people found a political voice. These determinants do not represent an alternative to the focus on economic and social factors in the old analysis. Rather, they constitute a link between politics and society. What we offer here is an attempt to re-think class-centred history, drawing on the logic of recent revisionist literature and suggesting some of the possibilities of a polity-centred approach. Subsequent chapters will discuss how political identities could be constructed in relation to other factors such as gender, race and nation.

THE STATE

The old analysis tended to relate the course of popular politics to changes in the economy. It was assumed that economic depression created a constituency for radicalism whilst economic recovery led to apathy. As William Cobbett remarked: 'I defy you to agitate a man with a full stomach'. By contrast, in a polity-centred interpretation, the nature of the state helps shape the character of popular politics. Whilst it is easy to assume that the state is unchanging or has an infinite capacity to create order, the reality is that the state is historically specific and historians need to appreciate its peculiarities because, as Theda Skocpol argues, the structure of the state plays a role in ' "selecting" the *kinds* of political issues that will come onto (or be kept off) a society's "political agenda" '.[1]

The structure of the eighteenth-century state was characterised by decentralisation. Britain's judiciary was independent and its elite was distinguished by its readiness to be bound by the law. The separation of powers between executive, legislature and judiciary was held to guarantee the liberty of the individual. Power was devolved to the local level. The basic unit of government was the parish where even the working class had some access to the state. Equally important were middle-class voluntary organisations which were active in providing solutions to social problems such as poverty. This was a 'reactive state', dependent on forces outside itself to provide social and economic reform.[2] During the nineteenth century, despite changes in state formation, most English people continued to feel that local matters were their own affair.[3] With the Sturges Bourne Acts of 1818 and 1819, the local franchise was restricted to owners of property. These ratepayers' democracies resented any interference from the growing state.[4] As David Eastwood puts it, 'power and authority within the English state were . . . the products of negotiation between the centre and the localities'.[5] Thus the devolved structure of the state shaped the agenda of popular politics which was characterised by opposition to centralisation.

This is crucial because, despite the importance of local government, the state was far from weak. Repeated warfare throughout the eighteenth century (from the War of Spanish Succession through to the Napoleonic Wars) had dramatically increased the power of central government through the levying of taxation and the introduction of a bureaucracy necessary to administer what John Brewer terms the 'fiscal-military state'.[6] In other words, what existed by 1815 was a decentralised but strong state. Popular politics in the nineteenth century wrestled with this particular form of state power. Radicals denounced what they called 'Old Corruption', the use of patronage with government run through placemen. 'Old Corruption' was seen as a threat to the independence of Parliament as MPs could be bought off with lucrative government jobs. The whole purpose of liberalism and radicalism was to rein in the excesses of the fiscal-military state which levied unjust taxes across the board in order to prop up a system of placemen and aristocratic privileges. Indirect taxation (such as duties on goods) particularly hit the working classes and therefore led to poverty. As 'Orator' Hunt put it at Spa Fields in 1816, 'What is the cause of the want of employment? Taxation. What was the cause of taxation? Corruption'.[7] The liberal solution took the form of retrenchment, demands for government accountability and a professional approach to affairs of state. Its language was that of the new political economy. Thus it was the state as much as embryonic class consciousness which shaped politics. The expansion of the franchise was required to make the state accountable and establish a fairer fiscal policy. This state-centred approach laid the basis for a political alliance between middle-class liberals and working-class radicals which came and went during the century but focused on the key liberal demand of free trade (a policy held to benefit the consumer). Faced with bloated state power, it is no surprise that popular politics of varying kinds opposed centralisation and adopted a fiercely individualist, sometimes almost anarchic, form. The state's intervention in the marketplace through the Corn Law of 1815 was a clear demonstration that government was a front for the landed elite, maintaining the high price of corn despite its social cost.[8] The same was true of the Combination Acts which attacked trade unions and were not repealed until 1824. The essentially repressive posture of the state from the 1790s to the 1820s determined that popular politics would take a class form, teaching diverse trades the need for solidarity and for a political diagnosis of economic ills.

In the 1820s, Lord Liverpool's government responded to widespread criticism by moving into its phase of 'Liberal Toryism', the purpose of which was to remove the state from the market by reducing duties on goods. This process of government withdrawal, which escalated over the next fifty years, was to be the hallmark of the *laissez-faire* state. The commitment to non-intervention was broadly retained by the Whig governments of the 1830s although they were prepared to countenance social reforms on a case-by-case basis. The patronage system that sustained 'Old Corruption' was gradually dismantled.[9] Whig and Peelite reforms in the 1830s and 1840s such as the 1842 Mines Act and the repeal of the Corn Laws both expanded and legitimated the state, suggesting that it was above class interests, thus discrediting radicalism, the essence of Stedman Jones' argument in 'Rethinking Chartism'.

William Gladstone's budgets in the 1850s set the seal on a quarter of a century of liberalism. He pursued a policy of retrenchment, abolishing many duties and reducing government expenditure, that limited the role of the state but also established a firm regulatory role for it. Gladstone followed his mentor, Peel, in fashioning a state structure which did not appear to discriminate in favour of any interest group at a fiscal level.[10] The moralised mid-Victorian liberal state was able to absorb popular demands through the extension of the franchise in 1867 and through trade union legislation in 1871 and 1875. The labour movement was then able to forge links with the state which led to the institutionalisation of class conflict. Trade unions operated after 1871 within state-sanctioned forms of collective bargaining.

However, the whole question of the liberalisation of the state depends on where one looks at the state from. For the Tolpuddle Martyrs, the participants in the 1839 Newport rising or the anti-Poor Law agitators, the state looked anything but liberal. The 1834 Poor Law Amendment Act, with its introduction of the despised workhouse system, was recognised as an assault on customary rights even though primarily it was locally administered. Its instigation led to alliances based largely on social class. Unsurprisingly, anti-Poor Law agitation fed directly into Chartism. V.A.C. Gatrell has described this period as witnessing the rise of the 'policeman state' in which the police force was developed largely to keep radicalism in check.[11] John Saville's *1848* dismisses talk of liberalisation as mere rhetoric. He argues that repressive state power (in the form of the police and the military) was needed to restrain the radical challenge in the year of revolution. The year 1848 represented the triumph of the capitalist state, consolidating the alliance between the aristocracy and the middle class whilst creating a social order in which the working class was disciplined.[12] Furthermore, if it is true that the state became more liberal in the nineteenth century (thus apparently determining the political agenda), it took a long time for news of this to filter down to the working class. In the 1870s, at a time when the state was apparently establishing itself as an impartial umpire between the classes, *Reynolds's Newspaper* (one of the most popular working-class papers) was still able to denounce the state as a racket for the aristocracy.[13] Some historians have wondered why radicals continued to attack the aristocracy rather than the middle class who had become the new ruling class by mid-century. The language of 'Old Corruption' retained its salience because the aristocracy continued to dominate society at most levels up to the end of the period under discussion.

The purpose of the mid-Victorian state was to promote *laissez-faire* economics and embody the interests of male property owners. However, in the 1880s and 1890s, Gladstone's liberal state received a series of shocks. The shift towards monopoly capitalism accompanied by concerns about economic decline unsettled the liberal belief in *laissez-faire*. Revelations abounded about the extent of poverty in Britain's major cities. The unemployed rioted in London's West End in 1887. The Woman Question (although not the dramatic issue that it was shortly to become in the Edwardian era) contested the masculine posture of politics whilst mass democracy challenged the essentially elitist nature of Liberalism. The state appeared close to being literally torn apart by the issue of Home Rule for Ireland. These shocks were to produce a crisis in liberal thought. Where formerly the state had been viewed as the enemy of freedom, the New Liberalism increasingly came to believe that state intervention was necessary in order to promote freedom, paving the way for the Liberal welfare reforms after 1906. This was also the period of the revival of socialism and the emergence of the New Unionism. A polity-centred interpretation might therefore see the rise of Labour not just as the product of a mature class society but also as the outcome of a crisis of legitimacy within the state.[14] Standard liberal solutions were failing, thus creating a space in which new ideas could enter the political agenda.

Clearly, it is necessary to bring the state back in so as to understand the peculiarity of political forms. However, this approach carries with it problems characteristic of the new revisionism. A state-centred approach tends to emphasise the essentially consensual nature of popular politics, focusing on the way in which similar forms of language were spoken across the social spectrum. For example, plebeian radicals and middle-class liberals from 1815 to *c.*1880 were both concerned about the excesses of the fiscal-military state but this does not mean that their aspirations were the same. Disputes about wages and the lack of representation at all levels of society could produce conflicts that took a class form. Alliances with the middle class were controversial because they risked the subordination of workers' interests to those of the bourgeoisie. For Feargus O'Connor, Chartism had to be an independent working-class movement in order to promote the interests of his followers. Consensus frequently broke down between radicals and liberals and had to be re-forged. Another problem with a state-centred reading is that it sees the working class as a pawn, its agenda subject to the complexities of state formation, which contrasts with E.P. Thompson's portrait of a class active in creating its own political culture. 'Top down' history can be deceptive.

Nevertheless, a state-centred interpretation does have its uses. Dislike of an unrepresentative state explains the overall course of popular politics in the second half of the nineteenth century, preferring self-help to state intervention. The campaign against the Contagious Diseases Acts (1870–86) launched by Josephine Butler was incensed by the capacity of the state to interfere with basic liberties. The Acts were an attempt to check the spread of syphilis in military towns through the compulsory inspection of prostitutes but, crucially, not their male clients. This was not just an example of the sexual double standard but it also suggested that the state had the power to intervene even at the level of the human body.[15] Thus it is not surprising that the welfare reforms passed by the Liberals after 1906 should have been greeted with suspicion by working-class people steeped in a dislike of state power. It was only particular reforms such as Old Age Pensions that were able to overcome this, and then usually only after they had come into effect.[16] The movement towards state-centred social reform represented a transformation for the labour movement which had previously been characterised by its support for independent voluntary organisations such as friendly societies.

Popular politics was therefore characterised by flight from state power in the period under discussion. The state's hostility to organised labour was interpreted by radicals in terms of class. It became necessary for working-class people to obtain the vote so as to remove the state's coercive role from the labour market. Political exclusion was the driving force behind class politics.

THE FRANCHISE AND THE PUBLIC SPHERE

The concept of the 'public sphere' was introduced into historical discourse by the philosopher Jürgen Habermas, who raised the question of how people came to think of themselves in collective ways.[17] He located a transformation in the seventeenth and eighteenth centuries where rational argument rather than status became the basis for decisions and the rising bourgeoisie began to have consciousness of itself as a 'public'. This led to the argument that all legitimate authority had to be derived from 'public opinion' (a related but distinct concept from the public sphere). One of the most obvious manifestations of public opinion in the nineteenth century was the demand for the vote. In the Marxist analysis, the working-class battle for the vote was part of its role as the agent of social transformation. Linking the franchise with the public sphere, we might conceive of the struggle for the franchise not simply as an expression of a new class consciousness but more profoundly as something that helped construct a working-class 'public'. It did not reflect a popular constituency; it actually created it, uniting people of diverse occupational and regional backgrounds that might not otherwise have considered themselves to have much in common. Revisionism sees this not as an inevitable development but as a complex process.

The role and nature of the franchise has become a much debated topic in recent years. Historians were writing against a background of concern about the decay of local government and a belief that the 'first past the post' system of elections was in decline with the failure of the opposition parties up to 1997 to defeat Conservative governments. If it is true that all history is contemporary history, then it is no surprise to find that historians have found new ways to think about the franchise and its impact on politics at a time when democracy itself was the subject of public debate. This section will show how the franchise determined the agenda of popular politics in much the same way as the characteristics of the state did. Indeed, the two are linked. Radicals saw aristocratic power as the problem. The radical achievement was to convince people that the solution to aristocratic domination was universal manhood suffrage.

'Democracy' did not acquire a positive meaning until the late Victorian period. Yet the vote and the democratisation of politics was the central aim of oppositional culture. The franchise was important because it determined the ability of people to be heard and played a part in defining classes. The 1832 Reform Act helped construct the middle class by defining it as those who had the vote.[18] At the same time, working-class identity was defined by its exclusion from the franchise. In 1867, Albert Venn Dicey argued that this was the reason for so much 'class feeling' among the working class: 'Treated as a class, they have fallen back upon their class feeling, and have devoted their energies to class interests.' Dicey perceived that the franchise provided a political identity and that constructing an identity based on citizenship rather than class would reduce social tension: 'A free extension of the franchise in 1867 will, in thirty years, make the artisans as little distinguishable from the rest of the nation as the men whose fathers in 1832 almost overthrew the Constitution from which they were excluded.'[19] Thus, the franchise is integral to a polity-centred interpretation because it generated class.

The conventional Whiggish account of the nineteenth century portrays a stately progression towards full democracy in stages (1832, 1867, 1884–5, 1918, 1928) cementing the Westminster model of representative government as opposed to direct democracy. The slow move towards democracy was interpreted as a series of concessions by the ruling class that were successful in that they staved off revolution. The middle class and then the working class were gradually incorporated into the polity. The creation of a mass electorate after 1867 and 1884–5 established a modern political system where parties vied with each other to provide social reform from which most people benefited. Moreover, the Reform Acts were part of a process of nation building. A more uniform franchise was essential to the creation of a sense of national identity and to a coherent public sphere. Although these developments have usually been seen in a positive light, historians have always pointed to the reactionary nature of Reform. The 1832 and 1867 Reform Acts were intended to preserve the political influence of the aristocracy (in which they were successful). The 1885

Redistribution Act privileged single-member, middle-class, suburban constituencies, constructing a political system based on class division that allowed for the growth of 'Villa Toryism'.

Recently, a new constitutional history has emerged that contests this account. The unreformed electoral system has been defended in a series of revisionist works.[20] Previously, the pre-1832 system was considered an indefensible chaos of corruption and bribery from which the majority of the population was excluded. However, J.A. Phillips and Frank O'Gorman have contended that such corruption was inevitable in an age without mass communications. Furthermore, in many seats the franchise was very wide and the size of the electorate was expanding. Many middle-class people and even members of the working class could vote. Some constituencies virtually had universal manhood suffrage, which was never the case after 1832. Hence the Great Reform Act halted what was already a potentially democratic system and replaced it with a franchise based on property alone.[21] For this reason, James Vernon considers 1832 to be a step back rather than a milestone on the path to mass democracy. Popular politics in the eighteenth century was in his view a public activity in which the crowd, although lacking the vote for the most part, was able to make its views known and had to be accommodated by the elite. The coming of mass democracy was part of the closing down of the public sphere in which the rough and rowdy political culture of the people was disciplined. Politics was privatised, taken away from the people and made specifically the preserve of middle-class males. This privatisation was completed through the secret ballot introduced in 1872 which addressed voters as private individuals rather than as part of a collective. Before 1832, constituencies had only one central polling place but the Reform Act provided separate polling booths for every 600 electors. Whilst this can be seen as more democratic, enabling greater ease in political participation, it made life more difficult for the disenfranchised crowd whose activities were dispersed across the constituency and whose collective power was thereby reduced. In effect, crowd activities were killed off by the repressive tolerance of liberalism.

The later Victorian franchise has also been the subject of much revisionism suggesting that it was more democratic than previously assumed. John Davis' study of the slum vote established that the lodger qualification of the 1867 Act was elastic and added many votes to the register. Duncan Tanner's study of the post-1884 electorate found that, although nowhere near universal, the franchise was very wide. Indeed, whilst there was an undeniable bias in the system against the working class, there was also a slight bias against the middle class because of the importance of the residency qualification. This there-fore casts doubt on the limited franchise as an explanation for Labour's relative lack of electoral success before 1918.[22] The franchise was both more and less democratic than had previously been assumed.

This new constitutional history (extending from Phillips and O'Gorman to Davis and Tanner) is extremely diverse but it qualifies or even destroys many Whiggish assumptions. The portrait that emerges is uneven and is particularly characterised by its distance from conven-tional arguments about class. Electoral divisions often did not reflect disputes over the economy. After 1867, working-class voters did not automatically create a working-class party. As we will continue to find in this book, there were other political identities that transcended class. Yet class remains stubbornly on the agenda. Workers entered the polit-ical arena defined in class terms, as well as by their gender (see Chapter Six). The franchise was not only integral to the creation of a masculine public sphere but it structured the whole culture of popular politics.

Nineteenth-century radicalism, however, cannot be reduced to the simple pursuit of the vote. Rather, it represented an attempt to democratise all levels of social life, from education to religion, expanding access to the public sphere.[23] The period between 1832 and 1867 saw a series of attempts by radicals to construct a virtuous working-class public sphere worthy of the franchise.[24] Respectability became a key radical virtue. The libertine ethos of artisan society in the early nineteenth century was abandoned in favour of sobriety and moral advance, countering the middle-class view that working men were irresponsible drunks. The rough culture of the common people, evident in elections, went into decline. Elections had previously been ritual events, splendidly evoked by Dickens in his account of the Eatanswill election in *The Pickwick Papers* (1837). Rituals included the ceremonial practice of 'chairing' (carrying the elected candidate through the streets), the wearing of party colours and bands playing popular songs such as 'See the conquering hero comes' as well as much alcohol and brawling.[25] By the 1870s, these rituals were in decline although they could still provide occasional opportunities for violence. Their place was taken by the party political machine which in turn was the expression of a more disciplined form of popular politics.

PARTY FORMATION

Today, the most obvious form of political identity is a party identity. It was not always so. A coherent mass-party system only emerged in the later nineteenth century, transforming the nature of popular politics and redirecting concerns from local to national issues. Party activities and organisations changed politics from something that took place according to the vagaries of the electoral cycle into an ongoing activity. Newspapers increasingly declared their loyalties to one of the main parties, thereby acting as an additional spur to viewing politics through the lens of party as did the cult of party leaders such as Peel and Gladstone.

Although the nineteenth century saw the formation of a party system, it was, ironically, a period when the idea of party was detested. In the eighteenth century, the common demand had been for 'Measures not Men'. In other words, MPs were expected to vote on the issues in a disinterested way and not because of instructions either from a party or a patron. The whole idea of a party contradicting the government for the sake of opposition was dismissed as immoral; hence the key political terms that lasted into the following century were 'independence' and 'patriotism'. Party voting suggested a narrow, selfish view of the world. Independence meant freedom from clientage and sectional interests. Indeed, nineteenth-century elections consisted of one candidate trying to pin a party label on his opponent whilst insisting on his own independence.[26] Anti-party was part of a wider distrust of the political process and popular attitudes towards politicians could often be very negative.[27]

The concept of a Member of Parliament was debated at a local level in the early nineteenth century. Edmund Burke had argued that an MP was not bound to present the views of his constituency in Parliament but simply had to speak the truth as he saw it. Nineteenth-century radicals contested this view in some constituencies, insisting that an MP was a delegate of the people rather than a representative.[28] The Chartist demand for annual parliaments was not an eccentric proposal (usually dismissed as a curiosity today). In its time it was an integral part of the Chartist vision, providing for accountability and delegate democracy. However, the view of the MP as a representative won out as the century wore on.

Until recently historians tended to downplay the importance of ideology in politics during the eighteenth century, interpreting parties mainly as interest groups. Through the influence of the new intellectual history (and especially J.G.A. Pocock) there has been a greater tendency to take ideology seriously.[29] The party identities of Whig and Tory date back to the Exclusion Crisis of 1678–81 and were given meaning by the Glorious Revolution of 1688. Whigs supported the contractual monarchy of William and Mary and defined politics as an essentially secular pursuit. Tories on the other hand viewed the new monarchs as de facto rulers instead of rulers by right. A party creed became the characteristic of the Rockingham Whigs in the 1760s as part of the assault on authoritarianism. The spirit of aristocratic Whiggism was then expressed by Charles James Fox who refined what became the 'Grand Whig' philosophy of disinterestedness and support for public opinion as long as it took a constitutional form. This contrasted with liberalism which stressed the new political economy and whose philosopher was Jeremy Bentham.[30]

After 1832, party loyalties in Parliament began to harden. Whigs and Liberals were associated with Reform and with cities; Tories were the party of the landed interest and of the counties. Even here, however, the distinction was not clear cut given the existence of many Whig landowners and Tory manufacturers and it was only in the broadest sense that parties existed. Party discipline was negligible and organisation in the country limited. Electoral politics continued to be dominated by the choice of a local patron or aristocrat.

The Reform Act of 1867 introduced an age of mass parties in which the political machine determined the content of politics. The Conservative and Liberal parties vied with each other to make increasingly ideological appeals to blocs of voters. The vote was not just determined by class or a view of the state but, quite simply, by what the electorate thought about a particular party's record. This called for new forms of electioneering. Attempts were made to familiarise electors with the rituals of Parliament.[31] Whilst the spin doctor was a thing of the future, image and presentation began to matter much more in politics. In the Bulgarian (1876) and Midlothian (1879) campaigns, Gladstone became the first politician to stump the country. Where politics had principally been a local matter, Gladstone helped create a national constituency that would be roused by his moralising of politics. After 1867, the Conservative Party created a network of Conservative Working Men's Associations. The Liberal defeat in 1874 led to the creation of the National Liberal Federation. What became known as 'caucus' politics was deeply disturbing because it appeared to threaten the independence both of the voters and of the candidates. However, the political machine was still at an early stage. Parties campaigned at elections on principles rather than clear programmes or policies. Hence the Liberal Party was able to maintain a wide alliance of Radicals, ex-Peelites and Whigs because it was united in admiration for the moral rectitude of Gladstone. Organised labour in particular distrusted formal party machinery, explaining in part the absence of a Labour Party until 1900.

At a parliamentary level then, there is clear evidence of party formation after 1832. However, if we define parties as national organisations, it was the 1867 Reform Act which gave rise to the modern party system (although there were traces of mass party formation before this). Historians of electoral behaviour assumed that party formation in late Victorian England mirrored the growth of class society. However, the penetration of party identities was uneven throughout the country. Support for the two main parties cut across the classes. Revisionists have begun to focus on the way in which political parties construct their own constituencies, rather than reflect them (appealing to diverse sectors of the electorate).[32] For revisionists, party politics cannot simply be reduced to class. Strategy has to be taken seriously. Mid-Victorian Liberalism enjoyed its success because it provided an identity that could appeal to a large part of the population, transcending class to some extent. The achievement of the Labour Party after 1900 was to actually create a class identity, overcoming differences of region, skill or gender. The significance of parties is not so much that they represented popular feelings but that they institutionalised those feelings and thereby transformed them.

POLITY-CENTRED HISTORY

Social history is now fractured with different areas having their own relative autonomy (language, politics, the state). Is there any way in which to bring the social and the political together? The 'relative autonomy of the political' is a creative insight that can enrich social history. Far from negating the importance of social structure, it draws attention to the way in which economic and social life is transformed into collective action. What is problematic is any polity-centred interpretation that moves towards 'the total autonomy of the political', that neglects social structure in favour of old fashioned political history, where Westminster is seen as a self-enclosed world answerable to no one. Whilst this is no doubt how it seemed to many contemporaries (and possibly still does), we need to situate parliamentary politics within the wider network of power. Revisionism is weak on the human dimension of popular politics. Employing methods from intellectual history involves taking the working class out of history. Ideas come to stand for people and their complex motivations. It is not just language that turns people into political actors. Much depends upon the bonds of solidarity within the communities they inhabit. The advantage of the 'history from below' tradition associated with E.P. Thompson was that it demonstrated how working-class people had agency, how they could create their own culture despite many constraints. Politics therefore needs to be understood in its broadest sense.

Revisionism, despite its sensitivity to the state, also neglects the reality of state power, which severely constrained the activities of popular radicals. Paul Pickering's collective biography of Manchester Chartist leaders reveals that most radicals in the early Victorian period could expect to spend a considerable amount of time in jail.[33] Politics was, quite simply, dangerous. Revisionism views political motivation in a simplistic manner. People became political in different ways depending on context. This could take the form of a mass meeting addressed by a charismatic speaker or it could take the form of incendiarism and threatening letters to local employers in rural areas. What is necessary then is a more expansive view of politics that takes culture and gender into consideration, as in Chapter One where the benefit of a multi-layered, complex approach to politics was presented. Revisionism suffers from a rather one-dimensional reading of historical evidence, privileging the written word in an age (before 1870) when many people could not read. For example, Paul Pickering has drawn our attention to the importance of the visual within Chartism. When Feargus O'Connor was released from York Castle in 1841, he chose to wear fustian, the clothing of the working man, which Pickering argues was seen by the crowd who gathered to greet him as a statement of 'class without words'.[34]

By concentrating on resources for organisation or the way in which political language was able to make sense of social problems, revisionism has rightly rendered problematic the way in which people become political. Here is the opportunity to reconnect the political to the social: any political strategy only succeeds through the effectiveness of its diagnosis of social structure. Thus political strategy needs to be inserted back into social history and politics itself should be seen as part of the life of the community.[35]

Far from banishing class analysis, revisionism may prove to be a way of keeping class on the historical agenda. Whilst popular movements emerged from the working class and were animated by the tensions of an unequal class society, they were also influenced by political determinants which gave them their character. Let us take the March of the Blanketeers. In 1817 impoverished weavers and others from Lancashire launched a hunger march to protest against their social distress. They marched south to present petitions to Parliament, carrying their blankets with them (hence the name) and hoping to gather support along the way. The authorities ensured that the marchers were dispersed well before they reached London. There is a clear link in this episode between economic factors (poverty) and working-class politics. However, the form of protest employed was not just the hunger march, it was also the petition (a form sanctioned by Parliament). From the start of the nineteenth century, popular politics absorbed much of the culture of Westminster. This was evident in the ways in which petitions were framed. It was important that they took a properly constitutional form so that they could be at least presented to Parliament. Improper wording meant that a petition would not be heard.[36] The petition proved to be an enduring form among the working class, particularly in the form of Chartism. Thus the Blanketeers episode is not just about the inequalities generated by industrial capitalism. It also tells us how politics played a transformative role in constructing the way in which social demands were expressed. A polity-centred approach expands our understanding of social history.

The revisionism discussed in this chapter and the last has pointed to the essential strangeness of politics. The political realm often limited and institutionalised social tensions but also played an enabling role in providing explanations of distress and constructing strategies to deal with it. Taking politics seriously is then a way of taking society seriously. The peculiarity of politics is that it alerts us to the complex process by which ordinary people found a voice.

5 The culture of popular radicalism I

Populism, class and the constitution

John Gast, whom we encountered in Chapter One as a supporter of
Queen Caroline, was the leader of the Thames shipwrights for most of
the early nineteenth century. Little is known about him. We glimpse
him in the pages of I.J. Prothero's study of his life and times practising
his craft in the shipyards of Deptford, a self-educated artisan making a
living in the difficult economic circumstances that followed the
Napoleonic wars.[1] Yet this shadowy figure was one of the most significant leaders of the early trade union movement. He helped lead the
shipwrights' strikes in 1802 and 1825. In 1818, he became president of
the 'Philanthropic Hercules', a shortlived attempt at an all embracing
metropolitan trade union. He was also identified by the Home Office
that year as a leading radical reformer. Gast participated with Francis
Place in the successful campaign to repeal the Combination Acts in
1824 and was later active in the co-operative movement and the
National Union of the Working Classes.

The radical artisan has become a key figure in the literature on
popular politics. Skilled workers often differentiated between themselves and the rest of the working classes, insisting on their honour
and respectability, something that manifested itself in corporate as well
as individualist forms. Artisans formed trade unions and paid into
friendly societies for security against accident, sickness and care in old
age. Although opposed to drunkenness, respectability for Gast meant
independence rather than morality. At one time a dissenting preacher,
he later joined the freethinking secularist circles that flourished in
London and was interested in both rational religion and fortune
telling. Amongst the working classes, it seemed natural for artisans to
take the lead in political activity as they tended to be the most literate
members of the community. Gast wrote a number of political
pamphlets and was associated with trade union newspapers such as
The Gorgon (1818–19). His ideology derived from a set of ideas that

had cohered in the writings of Thomas Paine in the 1790s. Paine's *Rights of Man* was not only a defence of the French Revolution but set the radical agenda for the following hundred years by mixing the elite Country Party ideology which had been the chief language of opposition with the egalitarianism of the artisans. Paine's supporters considered themselves 'free-born Englishmen' who were opposed to what became known as 'Old Corruption', government by patronage and bribery. Artisans blamed their problems on an unaccountable executive that oppressed the working classes through taxation. At that time taxes were mainly obtained through customs duties on goods which hit the poor hardest. Yet there was nothing the poor could do about it as Parliament was elected by a minority of the population. Paine located government as a parasite on the people and taxes as a form of robbery. Labour became the main source of value. Virtue rested with those who worked and produced things. Those who did not (aristocrats, courtiers, government placemen) were leeches on society. Artisan radicals argued that their skill constituted a form of property and therefore earned them the right to vote. These democratic views were clustered together in the mass platform. The mentality of Gast's generation was therefore shaped by a democratic and egalitarian inheritance from the revolutionary underground of the 1790s.

If political identity was shaped by the forces discussed in Chapter Four, does that mean there is no room for social explanations of politics? What we learn from Prothero is that whilst the political context played a decisive role, political activism emerged from the experiences of the labouring classes. The ideology of radicalism only drew support when it made sense of economic grievances and allied them to a political strategy (in the period after 1815, the demand for parliamentary reform). Politics and culture mediated popular experience and transformed it into a movement. The economic dimension is therefore not irrelevant. For example, the study of popular politics has had to engage with recent historiography that has portrayed the nineteenth-century workforce as heavily fragmented. Mass production and the factory system were not dominant until the second half of the century. It makes more sense to talk about the 'working classes' rather than the 'working class'. In assessing the ideology of radicalism, we must remember that it spoke to a heterogeneous workforce which often did not think in terms of natural class alliances. But how was it able to do this? We have to insert political strategy into social and economic history.

Recent historians have found that class and class consciousness are not sufficient explanations by themselves for understanding the culture of radicalism. Instead they have employed terminology that transcends class: populism, constitutionalism, republicanism. This chapter and the next will explore the ways in which we need to re-think the traditional categories through which radicalism has been interpreted.

THE QUESTION OF POPULISM

The drift from class has involved a movement away from the desire to see radicalism as some form of proto-socialism. Instead, historians have tried to evaluate radicalism on its own terms and have increasingly turned to the concept of 'populism'. The language of populism apparently helped construct political constituencies throughout the century far more effectively than the language of class.

Until recently, 'populism' was a term rarely applied to Britain partly because the British were believed to have produced orthodox class politics and partly because no one could agree on what the word actually meant.[2] It was originally coined to describe the philosophy of the American People's Party, founded in 1892, although it has since been used to describe all radical agrarian movements in the United States from the end of the Civil War to 1900. The term was also employed to describe the (wholly unrelated) philosophy of Russian Socialism in the same period. But the use of the term spun out of control as it was applied to a variety of movements around the world from the philosophy of Mahatma Gandhi to the strategy of the Ku Klux Klan. 'Populism' in this sense means any form of politics that seeks a popular base for its policies. It usually takes the form of a belief in the basic goodness of the people who are perceived as threatened by sinister elites. The classic populist argument is the conspiracy theory. However, a term that has been used to describe Zapatistas in Mexico and Thatcherism in Britain is so elastic that it can include any form of politics in the modern era.[3] It is not surprising that many historians have been reluctant to employ a term that contains so little analytical precision but this has begun to change. Craig Calhoun and Patrick Joyce have both applied it to nineteenth-century Britain as an alternative to 'class' politics.[4] Calhoun defines 'populism' as a community-based form of radicalism. Arguing that 'the consciousness of *a class* need not be the consciousness of *class*', Joyce draws attention to non-class identities which he calls 'populist'.[5] The use of the term, 'the people', in popular discourse had multiple meanings that included class but, crucially, transcended it with its patriotic and religious resonances that also drew on the spirit of Romanticism. Populism, for Joyce, includes hostility to the aristocracy and the state as well as the wide appeal of politicians such as Gladstone. In his more recent work, Joyce has moved away from 'populism' (which his critics noted was very similar to the old category of 'class') and has investigated the spirit of 'demos' or the democratic imagination.[6] He has explored how people came to think in 'social' terms and has attempted to reconstruct the 'political imaginary' of the nineteenth century by thinking about how democracy came to be imagined in the first place. It was language and culture that made sense of political life. For example, as we saw in Chapter One, the resources of melodrama structured popular responses to Queen Caroline. Radicals rushed to the defence of a wronged woman.

Given the elasticity of 'populism', it is tempting to dispense with it as meaningless, given its lack of historical specificity and the fact that it was not a contemporary term. However, 'populism' does have its uses if it is seen not as an ideology but as a distinctive style in politics. Indeed, at one level, there was no such thing as 'populism', only populist rhetoric which derived from a space in popular culture that cannot be defined through the labels of 'left' and 'right'. The latter originated in the French Revolution but both are mainly twentieth century in usage. 'Populism' represented the point of intersection between popular culture and formal politics. This encounter was characterised by a political style that was ambiguous, untheorised and heavily dependent on the symbolic. In the nineteenth century, the encounter was expressed by the popular motif of the 'freeborn Englishman' and his rights. Gast and his fellow artisans venerated the lifestyle and common sense of the ordinary working man who wanted to be free from outside interference so that he could look after his wife and children. Populist radicalism was founded on the belief that the freeborn Englishman was under siege from forces that he could not control, particularly unjust taxation perpetuated by an aristocratic oligarchy answerable to no one but itself. Other forms of unwelcome outside interference included the military (opposition to a standing army) and Jewish financiers who were blamed by William Cobbett among others for the growing National Debt.[7] Implicit in the idea of the 'freeborn Englishman' was a celebration of patriarchy and the nation. This was a mythology that underscored the whole of popular politics. So ambiguous was the populist style that it could be appropriated by both Liberal and Conservative Parties in the later nineteenth century.

The key expression in the populist vocabulary was 'the people', a useful term because of its essential ambiguity. Who were 'the people'? The term was never stable and had multiple meanings. In the early part of the century, it was used to refer to the heavily restricted electorate, but the essayist William Hazlitt assigned it a different meaning in 1818 by associating it with those concerned with 'common and equal rights'.[8] By the 1830s, *The Pioneer* could demand the inclusion of the working class in the term:

> Those who call themselves the liberal statesmen of the present day, must go progressively with the people, but in the word PEOPLE (a word much misunderstood) they must, brethren, include *us*, the productive labourers, for what are the people without us?[9]

Radicals like William Benbow and Feargus O'Connor claimed to support 'the people'.[10] The language of the 1842 Chartist petition deployed the term continually as a synonym for the labouring classes.[11] Yet 'the people' at other times could also include the middle classes. Such lack of precision accounts for its durability. The term was not threatening, unlike 'the masses' which had sinister connotations.[12] Only selfish and unpatriotic elites could be against 'the people'.

We have already encountered one example of populism in the Queen Caroline affair. Although the Caroline agitation was an effective platform for radicals to maintain their political struggle, the class dimension was muffled by a stress on the people and on the nation. In a standard populist device, radicals claimed there was a conspiracy against the queen to deprive her of her just rights. The Green Bag in which evidence against the queen was delivered to Parliament during her trial came to represent all that was secretive and duplicitous about the elite. A pamphlet by William Benbow urged:

> Englishmen! You who love Fair Play and Open Trial, now open your eyes and read! Green Bags, SEALED UP, were sent to Parliament about the queen.[13]

The criticisms of Behind Closed Doors politics as opposed to open political behaviour were a constant thread in the populist style. The cause embodied the paradoxes of populism. It was simultaneously republican and monarchist, subversive and deferential. The agitation addressed a form of popular culture that resisted formal political programmes and was suspicious of the claims of elite politicians. Populist literature thrived on the exposure of scandal amongst the upper classes because it served to emphasise the basic goodness of the people. Working-class pleasure was also intrinsic to the populist style. Beef and beer appeared in much political iconography. In a broadside of 1870 urging electors to vote for the radical George Odger in Southwark, the lines ran:

Then send him into Parliament,
To put a stop to their capers,
And tell them we want a good beef steak,
Instead of herrings and taters.[14]

The populism of pleasure was central to the Conservatives' electoral strategy in the late Victorian period but it can also be found in the support for the Whig Lord Palmerston in the 1850s.

'Populism' is therefore a rather messy concept but we are not close to finding a better one. Anything that does not fit into a strict dichotomy between left and right is consigned to the dustbin of populism, accounting for the variety of political movements that bear the name. The populist style provided meaning in a disorderly world. Moralistic, sentimental and patriotic, it anchored radicalism within the culture of the common people. Its language often overlapped with that of class but its emphasis on 'the people' transcended it.

There are two levels to popular politics. The first is that of formal politics (political parties, the ideology of radicalism, etc.). The second level is comprised of informal politics. This would include the emotionalism and carnivalesque spirit of popular culture as well as traditional forms of protest. The language of populism was generated when these two levels met. Popular politics in the early nineteenth century was comprised of a series of intermittent encounters between these two levels, particularly 1816–20, 1830–2 and 1838–48. The rise of mass political parties in the second half of the century allowed for a more enduring engagement between popular culture and formal politics. Championing 'the people' rather than a single class helped build constituencies. The populist style became integral to the vocabulary of every politician who wished to generate a large base of support.

CONSTITUTIONALISM AND REPUBLICANISM

It is impossible to underestimate the significance of the constitution in popular politics, especially as it provided a political theory for the populist style.[15] Although the English constitution was (and is) unwritten, it was nevertheless believed to uphold the rights of the free-born Englishman (especially free speech and assembly). Nineteenth-century radicalism was the heir to the classical republican tradition which flourished in the Country Party ideology of the eighteenth century. Radicalism was not usually republican in the sense of aiming to abolish the monarchy. Rather, it believed in the balanced constitution established in the Bill of Rights of 1689 following the

Glorious Revolution. This divided power between the monarchy, the House of Lords (representing the aristocracy) and the House of Commons (representing the people). Such a system entailed a system of checks and balances through which any one part of the constitution could be restrained by the other two if it became too powerful. The outcome, it was believed, were the liberties of the freeborn Englishman. Thus some Liberal electoral songs in the 1860s actually described William of Orange as one of the architects of British radicalism.[16] This tradition was inspired by the ancient republics of Greece and Rome and received further encouragement from the American Revolution which put republican principles into practice. The theory of checks and balances formed the basis of the American Constitution of 1787. Within British history, Magna Charta and the revolutions of the seventeenth century were the key moments when restraints had been established on arbitrary royal power. The republican tradition therefore prized decentralised power as a prerequisite for liberty, accounting for its individualist and anti-statist tendency. This view contrasts with that of Thomas Paine who attempted to frame his argument in proper Enlightenment fashion on the existence of natural law and natural rights, rather than on historical precedent. However, so pervasive was constitutionalism that even Paine was unable to resist its attraction and framed much of his argument in its terms.

Apart from decentralisation, republicanism emphasised popular sovereignty and participation. Radicals in particular looked back to ancient Saxon liberties for an historical precedent which justified the right to vote. The Anglo-Saxon constitution was held to have been essentially democratic, based on the participation of the whole community. Looming large in the radical demonology was the 'Norman Yoke', an argument that had been revived in the seventeenth century and served as the basis for radical polemic right up to the late nineteenth century.[17] Quite simply, the Norman Yoke argument held that the land had been stolen from the English in 1066 when William the Conqueror had given it to his French barons. Their descendants, the modern aristocracy, were essentially usurpers. Worse, the Normans had suppressed the Anglo-Saxon constitution in which all could vote. Thus the Norman Yoke not only lent radicalism the grandeur of historical precedent but it also suggested that the basic political identity of the English was democratic. It blamed economic problems on the aristocracy rather than the new middle class. The Chartist G.W.M. Reynolds attacked William the Conqueror as the son of Carlotta ... a notorious prostitute – the English word 'harlot' being derived, it is said, from her name .... Property in the case of the Norman aristocracy was acquired by rapine, murder and violation of all laws, both human and divine; that property has descended by title of heirship down to the holders of the present day; these holders are the descendants of robbers and wholesale plunderers; and the origin of property, therefore, held by many aristocratic houses boasting of their lineage is *robbery!*[18]

Even in the 1870s, the radical John De Morgan could attack the contemporary enclosure of common lands in these terms:

The Common has been seized and 'enclosed' by act of the Landlord Parliament .... It is this tyranny shod with iron that has trampled down the peasant from the yeoman to a pauper; that, under Norman tyranny, took the manure from the peasant, now takes his sheep, then his cows, then his common land, till he is left with nothing but his precarious wages.[19]

Integral to popular radicalism was its view of history, particularly its belief in a golden age before the intense inequality of the modern era. This age was sometimes located in Anglo-Saxon England or the period before enclosure, sometimes in the reign of 'Good Queen Bess' (Elizabeth I) or, in the case of William Cobbett, in England before the Reformation.[20] This could be viewed as an empty form of nostalgia but in radicalism the past became a form of political argument. The experience of the Commonwealth of the seventeenth century was particularly important as it was held to have laid the basis for modern democracy. Oliver Cromwell was consistently invoked as were the other heroes of the English Revolution such as John Hampden. These were the men who had challenged tyranny and centralisation. Moreover, the puritan basis for radicalism provided it with the idea of duty and a concern that evil wherever it emerged had to be confronted.[21]

Recent historians have tended to argue that most radicalism was an appropriation of constitutionalism, which shaped its language and premises. The Queen Caroline radicals presented themselves as defenders of the authentic constitution. Chartism was essentially a struggle over the meaning of the constitution. In her battle to repeal the Contagious Diseases Acts, Josephine Butler claimed that she was trying to restore the constitution which had been assaulted by state intrusion on women's bodies. One of her pamphlets was titled *The*

Constitution Violated (1871). The language of constitutionalism was everywhere.

The increasing historical work on constitutionalism might appear to be an example of the retreat from class analysis. However, James Epstein views constitutionalism as a narrative that could contain many (sometimes contradictory) meanings and a terrain on which class could be debated. In a sensitive study of the uses of the revolutionary Cap of Liberty, he found that the key terms of constitutionalism such as 'the people' and 'patriot' were indeterminate and could be appropriated by working-class groups thus giving them a class meaning. Epstein allows that there is no such thing as a pure class language or movement but shows that we cannot ignore the fact that the iconography of the Cap of Liberty (associated with the French Revolution) was particularly deployed by workers in Lancashire and Cheshire in the first half of the nineteenth century. Although the Cap of Liberty was not an English symbol, it was employed in an unembarrassed way by radicals alongside invocations of English constitutionalism. Its re-emergence at popular meetings in 1819 struck terror into the hearts of the local magistracy. At the meeting that led to the Peterloo massacre, red caps of liberty were much in evidence. The local yeomanry made a point of capturing and destroying them, such was their symbolic importance. The language of constitutionalism that went alongside the use of the Cap of Liberty represented the site of psychic resistance by working people to a social order over which they had no control.[22] No approach to politics that ignores class and social structure can therefore be wholly satisfactory.

The traditional language of radicalism could be stretched at times of social tension to encompass class. Silk weavers in Spitalfields found themselves threatened in 1823 by the repeal of government legislation that had laid down rules for the setting of piece rates and that upheld the value of their labour. In an unsuccessful campaign against repeal, weavers went beyond 'Old Corruption' to target the capitalists who had demanded the new legislation. They later complained that:

> [As] the artisan's power of labour is his only property, it is irreconcilable with every sense of justice, and of common right, that the incomes and property of all other classes should be protected, whilst the artisans and labourers alone are left a prey to be plundered by needy, rapacious and unprincipled employers.[23]

Class understandings therefore arose from the inequalities of the workplace. The Chartist Richard Pilling, charged with seditious conspiracy in 1843, explained his reasons for supporting Feargus

O'Connor not by invoking the People's Charter but by saying 'it was always a wage question and ten hours bill with me'. He concluded his defence by saying '... the masters conspired to kill me, and I combined to keep myself alive'.[24] Radicalism was no disengaged debate over political theory nor in practice did it distinguish between social and political demands. The rights of labour were as important to the Chartists as the rights of citizenship. Constitutionalism co-existed with serious attempts to question the social and political order.

The diverse range of occupations and incomes amongst the working class has led historians to uncouple radicalism from class consciousness. Differences of ethnicity, gender and region as well as the division between skilled and unskilled meant that it was difficult to unite the working class in an effective way. An analysis of exploitation at the point of production (the hallmark of a mature class consciousness) barely existed in the early nineteenth century.[25] Yet, as Dorothy Thompson shows, what was distinctive about Chartism was its ability to unite working people regardless of skill, region or ethnicity. Class was a unifying factor in the creation of a national movement.[26] Within the politically charged atmosphere of the Chartist years, a class-based analysis could emerge. Class was an integral part of radical culture but radicalism was also composed of other elements that are not reducible to class.

RETHINKING POPULAR RADICALISM, 1815–48

This section will explore the content of popular radicalism to explain its appeal. A distinction should be made between parliamentary and popular radicalism. In Parliament, Radicals usually associated with the Whigs and employed the constitutional vocabulary of checks and balances. They stressed the increased representation of 'interests' (particularly urban workers) rather than individuals. Thus one enduring Radical demand was for equal electoral districts to counterbalance the aristocracy. Popular radicalism, however, went beyond this to demand household or universal suffrage.

Historians no longer tend to see popular radicalism as invariably anti-capitalist although, at its most extreme, radical culture held out the promise of an alternative form of society, as expressed in Owenism. For the most part, the existence of the good employer was always allowed by radicals and private property respected. The chief demand of trade unions was fairness, embodied in the slogan, 'A fair day's work for a fair day's pay', hallmark of a labourist consciousness. Radicals usually did not denounce the middle classes as capitalists but as supporters of legislation that oppressed the people, a position that left open the possibility of class collaboration. Exploitation was rarely located in economic production although Bronterre O'Brien's writings in the 1830s did mark a breakthrough to a new class explanation for exploitation.[27] The basic economic theory of radicalism was the labour theory of value. Radicals like John Gast believed the value of a commodity was determined by the amount of labour that went into it.

Commencing with Thomas Spence in the 1790s, radicals frequently advocated nationalisation of the land in order to break the monopoly of the aristocracy. Land reform was a standard aspect of the radical repertoire, evident most notably in the Chartist Land Plan.[28] A good example of radical continuity, it became in various forms part of the Liberal Party programme up to 1914. Although radicalism was not particularly collectivist, maintaining an energetic support for individual liberty, it could extend to demanding government intervention. Late Chartism was distinctive for importing socialist ideas from the French Revolution of 1848, including legislation to counter capitalist competition.[29]

In recent years, the culture of radicalism has received extensive treatment. The key theme has been the rise of respectability. Previously, the tendency was to see respectability as an example of bourgeois values dripping down to the working class, often as a form of social control. In this view, the success of the Victorian bourgeoisie was that it managed to disseminate the values of sobriety and thrift, leading to a pacific and unthreatening working class. The mid-Victorian belief that respectable values had taken hold of the working class allowed for the Reform Acts of 1867 and 1884 which created mass democracy. However, historians are now more inclined to argue that respectability emerged from within plebeian radicalism. Respectability was always a dimension of artisan politics, although as we saw in Chapter One, there was a strain of what Iain McCalman calls 'unrespectable radicalism'.[30] Radical journalists such as William Benbow inherited the eighteenth-century vogue for crude satire. Satirical prints featuring bawdy imagery and low humour were an essential part of the radical assault on 'Old Corruption'. Radicals such as George Cannon combined the publication of political tracts with pornography. Following in the tradition of Paine's *Age of Reason* (1794–6), many radicals were opposed to organised religion and secularism became a leading strain in oppositional thought.[31] However, the unrespectable dimension to radicalism went into decline in the early Victorian period. The use of crude satire was abandoned and leaders such as William Lovett protested their respectable credentials. Respectability became an essential aspect to the demand for social reform, linking the Chartists with the trade union junta of the mid-Victorian period who emphasised their undeniable respectability when lobbying for the labour laws. Where radicals at the beginning of the period under discussion were often in tune with the carnivalesque and bawdy dimension of popular culture, radicalism by the end of the century had frequently become disdainful of popular culture and eager to reform it.[32] Respectability had its price. The high moral tone of radicalism (or liberalism and socialism) frequently cut it off from large sections of the working class, creating a political space that was occupied either by apathy (the feeling that politicians were crooks, the belief in 'Them' and 'Us', the argument that voting does not change anything) or by popular conservatism as discussed in Chapter Eight.

Underpinning the rise of respectable radicalism was religion, particularly nonconformity. It is now difficult to conceive of radicalism without identifying the nonconformist conscience at work. From 1912 when Elie Halévy argued that Methodism had pacified the working class during the Industrial Revolution, historians have tended to see religion either as a form of social control or simply to dismiss its significance. Yet modern studies increasingly support the view that nonconformity underpinned artisan radicalism, providing it with a belief in the virtue of the common people and a conviction that Christians had to agitate for social reform. While Methodism may have pacified the revolutionary fervour of the working class, it also taught it how to organise. Moreover, its offspring, Primitive Methodism, produced a form of plebeian politics that sharply challenged the social order. Shunning, or sometimes excluded from, churches or chapels in the early nineteenth century, adherents met in fields and looked forward to the Second Coming of Jesus Christ as foretold in the Book of Revelation, a belief known as 'millenarianism'. The millennium that Jesus Christ would inaugurate was characterised by the perfect equality of human beings. This radicalised the supporters of the many millenarian sects and cults as it offered a critique of the inequality of social relations on earth.[33] Chartism inherited this millennial philosophy. An imprisoned Stockton Chartist explained that he became a Chartist because Jesus Christ was the first Chartist.[34] Chartists were infused with religious values and premises. The first editor of the *Northern Star*, William Hill, was a Swedenborgian minister. A common form of protest was a march to a local church where supporters took over the pews and demanded that the minister preach on the People's Charter. Radical culture was based on the values of the chapel as opposed to the Church. Hence political discourse was constructed by anti-clericalism. Not necessarily synonymous with atheism, anti-clericalism represented an assault on the domination of the Anglican church in all aspects of society. With its appeal to nonconformity, it became an essential part of popular liberalism.[35] The key to liberalism as well as radicalism was religious liberty as much as civil liberty.

The debate over respectability has been particularly focused in the historiography of temperance. The diffusion of the values of sobriety might be seen as a classic example of middle-class interference with working-class pleasure. Explanations of this kind usually stress middle-class status anxiety. However, although the original temperance advocates were middle-class, the movement was quickly taken over by workers. Brian Harrison has convincingly shown that temperance advocates were genuine social reformers, trying to deal with a deep problem in working-class life.[36] The image of the battered wife and children starving while their father drank his wages, so beloved of Victorian melodrama, was a lived reality in many homes. The temperance tradition became part of popular liberalism creating a groundswell of support for licensing legislation. However, in radicalism it constituted part of the deep moralism of Victorian politics, an assertion of the dignity of working-class manhood. Allied to this was an emphasis on knowledge and education. One of the standard arguments against democracy was the view that the working classes were not sufficiently educated and informed to exercise the vote. Many plebeian radicals such as William Lovett accepted the premises of this argument and encouraged the diffusion of useful knowledge and, particularly, literacy. The self-taught working man was too worthy and respectable to be denied the franchise.

In the 1970s and 1980s, historians began to take the form of radicalism seriously, particularly the mass platform and traditions such as radical dining and toasts. For example, Ashton radicals often held celebrations in honour of the birthdays of Paine and Hunt and commemorated Peterloo. The emergence of the annual works dinner in the 1850s signalled the end of this tradition and a move towards greater class conciliation.[37] Ritual was integral to radical culture, constructing a usable past and deploying symbols that made sense of the social order. Early Victorian radicalism became a way of life, based on public meetings, tea parties, newspapers such as the *Northern Star* and, in some areas, co-operative stores. Popular politics became a profession for the first time. The 'trade of agitation' led many radicals to abandon their normal employment (usually in one of the skilled trades) for a precarious career combining lecturing, journalism and bookselling. Professional agitators could find themselves selling all sorts of unlikely items such as Chartist scarves and even Chartist pills which promised 'to avert much of the illness usually affecting the working classes'.[38]

Integral to the creation of a working-class public sphere was the radical press, for example, the *Poor Man's Guardian* (1831–5) or *Reynolds's Newspaper* which commenced publication in 1850 and lasted till 1967, blending sensational stories with political polemic. The press helped generate a movement culture, the awareness of belonging to a movement. For example, the Chartist *Northern Star* featured reports from local groups and therefore reinforced the individual's sense of belonging to a wider political community. Issues were almost always handed around from person to person and illiteracy was not a barrier to consuming the paper's contents as articles were frequently read aloud. Many papers published the writings of working-class poets, asserting the civilised and respectable ambitions of the people.

Perhaps the most distinctive feature of recent historiography on radical culture has been the way in which the demagogue is now taken seriously. Historians formerly argued that demagoguery was the sign of an immature politics. Feargus O'Connor in particular has been blamed for hijacking Chartism and bringing about its demise. John Belchem's biography of Henry Hunt and James Epstein's study of O'Connor have effectively revised this view.[39] Instead, the demagogue is now seen as a natural part of the mass platform. Politics has never been immune to the cult of personality. If we are now to see popular politics on its own terms, then the charisma of the demagogue needs to be taken seriously. The objection that is usually made is that leaders were often middle-class and therefore unable to share the class interests of their followers. This view usually goes with the claim that radicalism failed because it was stabbed in the back by its leadership. What has now emerged is that leaders such as Hunt and O'Connor integrated and focused popular politics, providing it with narratives of martyrdom and struggle. Indeed, it was the cult of leadership that helped construct a following for radicalism. Many demagogues doubled as journalists, intensifying their relationship with the rank and file. William Cobbett, for example, not only wrote political tracts but provided followers with advice on gardening and how to court the opposite sex. Demagogues gave politics coherence. This was particularly true of the most unlikely demagogue of all – William Gladstone.

FROM RADICALISM TO LIBERALISM, 1848–1900: THE CONTINUITY DEBATE

As documented in Chapter Two, the old analysis tended to interpret the nineteenth century in terms of discontinuity. The radicalism of the post-1815 period was seen as immature, superseded by the new class awareness of Chartism. Following the defeat of Chartism in 1848, radicalism degenerated into support for liberalism, a betrayal of working-class interests. Only in the late nineteenth century did a new class consciousness emerge with the spread of socialism and the rise of Labour. However, this reading of the past has been contested. The new view suggests that there was an enduring continuity in radicalism. Stedman Jones, as we have seen, demonstrated that Chartism was essentially a continuation of eighteenth-century republicanism. I.J. Prothero showed that William Benbow's advocacy of a general strike in 1832 was not an example of early socialism but was rooted in traditional radicalism.[40] The emergence of the trans-class Liberal alliance was assumed to have begun in the 1850s, underpinning the social stability of the 'Age of Equipoise'. However, local studies of Bolton and Oldham have suggested that the roots of mid-Victorian consensus politics can be found as early as the 1830s, evident in the collaboration between working-class radicals and middle-class liberals. Severe class conflict was restricted to a short period between 1838 and 1842. More common was a cross-class commitment to democratic local government and the culture of self-improvement.[41] Biagini and Reid's revisionist collection, *Currents of Radicalism*, has argued that old radicalism continued to underpin popular politics up until 1914.[42] Rather than enjoying a status as an inferior form of socialism, radicalism was reclaimed by the contributors to the volume as a coherent and pragmatic approach to the problems of the age, feeding into the popular liberalism of the mid-Victorian period which has come into its own. Previously, it was assumed that radicalism had simply gone into decline after the Chartist failure of 1848, not to reappear until the 1880s. Liberalism was mainly considered to be a sign of the failure of independent working-class politics. Any form of radicalism whose inspiration was Gladstone appeared seriously deficient. Furthermore, the great study of popular liberalism by John Vincent denied that liberalism was an ideology or even a movement.[43] He saw it instead as a cluster of single issue pressure groups concerned with causes such as temperance (the United Kingdom Alliance), education (the National Education League) and parliamentary reform (the Reform League). This collection of groupings (often dismissed as faddists) only gained coherence through the figure of Gladstone. Popular liberalism was essentially irrational.

More recent historians, particularly Eugenio Biagini, have vindicated popular liberalism as a coherent philosophy based on the policy of 'liberty, retrenchment and reform'.[44] Not only was liberalism a continuation of the radical tradition defined in the last section, it was more successful than Chartism. Although a Conservative government extended the franchise in 1867, Liberals introduced the secret ballot and widened the county franchise in the Reform Act of 1884. This shift in popular politics was made possible by a greater confidence in the Westminster model of government following the repeal of the Corn Laws in 1846, the 1847 Factory Act and Gladstone's free trade budgets in the 1850s. Having accepted the tenets of free trade and political economy, trade unions were integrated into the liberal state through the labour laws of 1871 and 1875.

Biagini argues that liberalism cannot be explained through social structure but was instead based on a set of values that provided a more satisfactory form of identity than class. Liberals were committed to civil and religious liberties which set them apart from the Tories with their defence of the Anglican Church. They maintained the Whig reform tradition which was distinguished by its sensitivity to public opinion even though it was not democratic.[45] The cult of Gladstone was based on the belief that the state could be moralised. Cheap social reforms such as factory legislation did not contradict the general line that the state should not intervene. The liberal ethos prized local government, in which form it was prepared to countenance public ownership of major utilities. The architects of this popular liberalism were Richard Cobden, John Bright and Joseph Chamberlain. What existed therefore was a pragmatic but effective popular philosophy which made sense and was far from irrational. However, as Margot Finn has shown, the mid-Victorian years were also characterised by the radicalisation of the intelligentsia.[46] Leading liberal thinkers such as Frederic Harrison increasingly took on board many labour issues and moved towards a more positive view of state power. The labour movement created a fissure in classical political economy which prefigured both late Victorian socialism and the New Liberalism.

It is not therefore surprising that Chartists such as Robert Lowery should have become radical Liberals. Even Ernest Jones, one of the most radical Chartists, eventually found his way onto the Liberal platform, standing unsuccessfully for Manchester in the election of 1868. The basic tenets of radicalism and republicanism continued to inform politics in the mid-Victorian period. This continuity of radicalism could be expressed in unexpected or bizarre forms. In the 1870s and 1880s, the most popular working-class hero was the Tichborne Claimant, a butcher from Australia who claimed to be the long lost aristocrat Sir Roger Tichborne who had disappeared in 1854.[47] After two heavily publicised trials (1871–4), it was alleged that he was actually a man called Arthur Orton of Wapping and he was sent to prison as an impostor. Many working-class people believed that he was not only Tichborne but that he was a freeborn Englishman who could not get justice in a court of law. The Claimant was believed to be the victim of a conspiracy that included the wealthy Tichborne family, the government, the legal profession and sinister Jesuits. The Magna Charta Association, formed to defend him, also demanded triennial parliaments, votes for women and the abolition of duties on goods. Amongst the Claimant's supporters were the former Chartist G.W.M. Reynolds and Jack Williams, later a prominent member of the Social Democratic Federation. There were Tichborne newspapers, petitions and in 1875 the leader of the movement, Edward Kenealy, was elected to Parliament in effect as a Tichborne MP. Like the Queen Caroline agitation, the Tichborne movement stressed the virtues of 'the people' rather than class. Its ethos was constructed by the demand for justice and fair play. Supporters claimed that there was one law for the rich and one for the poor and upheld a civic virtue that needed protection from aristocratic elites over whom they had no control. The Tichborne case was a pastiche of previous forms of radicalism. Like the Queen Caroline agitators, Tichbornites carried on an old political tradition, the radical as blackmailer. They threatened to expose the terrible lives of the aristocracy which existed behind closed doors by showing how the Claimant was kept from his inheritance. By associating with an unrespectable figure like the Claimant, Tichbornites carved a position outside of liberalism which was always characterised by its essential respectability. More important than the formal politics to which it gave rise, the case expressed basic popular emotions about the social order. Hence the deep importance of motifs and symbols amongst supporters. For example, the Lord Chief Justice at the end of the trial argued that only 'fools and fanatics' could believe that the Claimant was innocent. Outraged supporters then took to describing themselves as 'fools and fanatics' on banners at meetings and in letters to the press. But was Tichborne political? The cause appropriated the language of radicalism with its concern for civil rights under the constitution and employed it to express popular hostility to the unequal nature of the law and social relations. We find in the Tichbornites' defence of customary morality a deep yearning for a just social order. Popular politics was never simply about parliamentary power. It was about the amount of control people had over their own lives.

Whilst there is a good case to be made for continuity, it is important to be sensitive to context. Although they had much in common, popular liberalism was not the same thing as Chartism. It did not contain an anti-capitalist dimension and it was founded on a more sanguine approach to the state than the Chartists evinced. Integral to Chartism was the prospect of social disorder and, even if the Chartists do not seem revolutionary to us, this is not how they were perceived at the time. There was a continuity both in terms of ideas and personnel but the context in which the movements operated was very different.[48] Examining radicalism and liberalism from a gender perspective also compels us to see the movements in very different ways.

6 The culture of popular radicalism II
Gender and socialism

GENDER POLITICS

Political identity is now more complex than used to be supposed. In the old analysis, it was common for identity to be discussed in terms of class consciousness or its absence. Hand in hand with this went the failure to examine women's lives. Since the advent of women's history in the 1970s, scholars have sought out women's contribution to politics and society so that it is now difficult to claim that they are 'hidden from history'. Sources are always a problem given that women's experience was often neglected by the mostly male-oriented sources historians employ for evidence. However, women's historians have overcome this by uncovering new sources such as diaries and forgotten books and tracts by women. They have also taken familiar sources (such as newspapers) and read them through the lens of gender. Although it has been criticised for ignoring women, E.P. Thompson's pioneering work in history from below opened up a space that women's historians have filled, providing a voice to those who have been silenced. New categories (such as separate spheres, melodrama and domesticity) have emerged to explain the content and course of popular politics. For example, the idea that the Chartists might have had a sexual politics was foreign to the old analysis. Gender may not be the only category of analysis but we now see that it was an important organising principle in the make-up of society.[1] No discussion of the culture of popular radicalism can therefore be complete without an examination of its gender dimension.

In Chapter One, we saw how the Queen Caroline agitation made little sense in terms of class but was comprehensible through the lens of gender. What happened to the female voice in politics thereafter? The dominant model which feminist historians have employed is that of separate spheres, the division of society into public and private that accompanied the Industrial Revolution. The public sphere was the world of work and of government (the male domain) whilst the private sphere was the world of the home (the female domain). Men and women had formerly worked together in rural industries but industrialisation led to the segregation of the sexes and women became identified with domesticity. Gender division therefore underpinned industrialisation. However, women were never successfully relegated to the home. In fact, the archetypal factory labourer was a woman, employed because she was cheap. Male workers frequently resented the way in which women were employed to undercut their wages and attempted to exclude women from the workplace.[2] The separation of the spheres was a model that was aspired to but was seldom achieved by workers. Recent debate among feminist historians has focused on the ways in which the division between public and private was never strict but was subject to contestation and re-negotiation in different historical circumstances.[3]

Although women were key participants in many political agitations, it is often difficult to recover their contribution from the historical record. At a (mainly) middle-class level, women were active in moral causes such as the campaign against slavery which also raised issues concerning female exploitation.[4] In the early part of the century, working-class women had been active in strikes and food riots. There were a number of female reform societies. The Hyde Female Political Union passed a resolution not to sleep with their husbands unless they supported the People's Charter. Given that a woman was allowed to be queen, female Chartists insisted that they therefore should have the right to the vote. In the Queen Caroline agitation, their activity was based not so much on class interests as on a wider defence of the community and of the family against a libertine king. This was characteristic of female protest. Women joined reform movements because of their role as wives and mothers. At a rally in Blackburn in 1819, Alice Kitchen of the Blackburn Female Reform Society complained:

> Our homes which once bore ample testimony of our industry and cleanliness ... are now alas! robbed of all their ornaments ... behold our innocent children! ... how appalling are their cries for bread![5]

According to Barbara Taylor, these kind of arguments both enabled and limited female participation by rooting women's politics in the sexual division of labour. Separate spheres defined female politics. The attraction of women to moral issues has led Sally Alexander to advise her fellow feminist historians to emancipate themselves from class.[6]

Women were usually excluded from hierarchical, class-based movements but were heavily involved in Owenite socialism.[7] The Owenite critique of marriage and its emphasis on a 'New Moral World' that transcended class proved hospitable to women's political activity in a way that artisan-dominated politics was not. Workshop production in the early nineteenth century lent itself to male camaraderie and even misogyny which not only excluded female participation but was characterised by its fear of cheap female labour.[8] Owenite feminists saw female oppression as trans-class although they also highlighted the exploitation of female wage labour. An editorial in the Owenite *Pioneer* (written by James and Frances Morrison) complained:

> A woman's wage is not reckoned at an average more than two thirds of a male and we believe in reality it seldom amounts to more than a third (and wives have no wages at all). Yet, is not the produce of female labour as useful? . . . The industrious female is well entitled to the same amount of remuneration as the industrious male.[9]

Owenism offered a profoundly different alternative to the sexual politics of early Victorian radicalism as we shall see.

The political activity of working-class women went into decline in the early 1840s. Some women adopted temperance and were therefore excluded from Chartist meetings that met in pubs. More fundamental was the shift from local to national politics during that decade. Political activism increasingly required travel and became focused on Westminster. This inevitably precluded women's participation because of the need to concentrate on their families and their problems of movement in the public sphere.[10] Women, by contrast, were active in the Chartist Land Company which seemed, like Owenism, to offer immediate redress to female concerns and in which women could participate at a local level.[11] Women also assisted in the political education of their children.

For middle-class women the story is the reverse. The mid-Victorian period saw many become politically active. Radical Liberalism provided a framework in which they could lobby Parliament for the vote. John Stuart Mill was prevailed upon to introduce an amendment to the 1867 Reform Bill that would have enfranchised women on the same terms as men. Although the amendment failed, it did put the issue of female suffrage on the political agenda. Significantly, when middle-class women did achieve political prominence in the second half of the century, it was through local government and especially School Boards to which women could be elected after 1869. That year, the municipal vote was extended to women, although *Regina* v.

Harrold (1872) determined that the franchise should only be extended to unmarried women ratepayers. In 1894, women were allowed to serve on parish and district councils but the right to sit on local councils did not come until 1907. Women also became Poor Law guardians in this widening of the public sphere. By 1900, women had become an integral part of local government. About a million enjoyed the municipal franchise.[12] However, only in the 1880s did women officially become part of the organisation of the hitherto exclusively male political parties. The Women's Liberal Federation was formed in 1887 after almost a decade of female activism on behalf of the party. The (Conservative) Primrose League harnessed female voluntary efforts from 1884 onwards. Political work was often considered unwomanly and activists continually had to negotiate with the ideology of separate spheres. Thus, Mrs. Wynford Phillips' *An Appeal to Women* (1890) on behalf of the Westminster Women's Liberal Association addressed its readers in the following terms:

> Women: your sphere is your home! Yes, but you have a double duty. First of all to your family, and secondly to the wider family, the world of human beings outside, and you fail in one of your most solemn obligations, if you devote yourself solely to your own home and your own children, unmindful of the fact that thousands of poor men and women have no homes . . . and that hundreds and thousands of little children are growing up uncared for, untaught, unthought of, in slums and alleys or the streets of our great cities.[13]

Female political activity in the second half of the century remained centred on moral issues. The most important of the mid-Victorian female campaigns were generated by concerns over sexuality. In the language of social reform the figure of the prostitute loomed large, an example of the way in which poverty undermined women's purity. Sexuality achieved prominence through the campaign against the Contagious Diseases Acts and the moral panic generated by W.T. Stead's 'Maiden Tribute of Modern Babylon', an exposé of child prostitution in the *Pall Mall Gazette* (1885).[14] The melodramatic dimensions of the latter case drove women and radical working men to demonstrate against aristocratic gentlemen believed to be preying on young girls. Their language employed the traditional themes of anti-aristocratic populism that we identified in the last chapter. The agitation resulted in the repeal of the Contagious Diseases Acts and the setting of the female age of consent at sixteen in 1886. This suggests that predominantly female political agitations could be more successful than masculine movements, partly because they transcended class.

Detailing women's contribution to politics is not enough. We need to think about the ways in which radical culture and the political process itself was gendered. Radicalism is increasingly being seen as a re-assertion of patriarchy, hence the need to think about its sexual politics. Citizenship was defined very much in masculine terms. In the early nineteenth century, it was not unusual for radicals to champion free love and birth control. However, the dominant strain in radicalism after the 1830s supported marriage and the traditional family, abandoning sexual egalitarianism in favour of the ideology of separate spheres.[15] The language of the freeborn Englishman was premised on the belief that the male labourer should work whilst his wife looked after his children. In his *Address to the Women of England*, the Whitby Chartist John Watkins praised the 'cottage of content' and claimed that women's work outside the home was a denial of their basic nature.[16] As with the Queen Caroline affair, radicals employed the language of chivalry, claiming that women were victims of sexual abuse by male overseers in factories. But, in fact, examples of sexual abuse in factories were relatively rare. Male Chartist concerns were therefore motivated by the loss of control over female labour and their sexuality.[17] These patriarchal concerns were maintained in the mid-Victorian period by the great demand of male trade unionists: the breadwinner wage.[18] The ambition of trade unionists was a wage that was sufficient for a man's wife to be able to stay at home. This was an alternative to organising women in the workplace. Radical politics essentially championed the independent male artisan. Domesticity was essential to radicalism, part of a process whereby politics was defined in increasingly masculine terms. For Anna Clark, 'the fatal flaws of misogyny and patriarchy ultimately muted the radicalism of the British working class'.[19]

Radicalism's focus on the vote set limits on the participation of women. Few radicals advocated anything as daring as female suffrage. Thus the struggle for the franchise involved the creation of an essentially masculine sphere from which women were excluded. Although the franchise was based on property, it was felt that working men possessed property through their skill. Female skill was not considered a form of property. The franchise was therefore a central part of patriarchy and the ideology of separate spheres. The 1832 Reform Act was the first to specifically limit the vote to men (although there is little evidence of women voting before this) and the right to vote became heavily tied to gender. The 1840s witnessed the growth of what Keith

McClelland calls 'the "masculinization" of popular politics'. In the debates preceding the 1867 Reform Act, radicals and trade unionists argued that working men should be given the vote as an integral part of their masculinity. Manly virtues (fortified by hard work which was so essential to masculine identity) would invigorate the political system. The Act gave the vote to urban male heads of household subject to a twelve-month residency qualification.[20] Masculinity was also integral to the debates on the introduction of the secret ballot in 1872 but in a different way. Opponents of the reform argued that voting in secret rather than in public was unmanly (and also unEnglish).[21] Whilst the vote was based on property and gender, after the broadening of the franchise in the 1884 Reform Act the vote was seen to be based less on property and more on gender. The fact that men alone could vote created a space that would ultimately be occupied by the suffragettes.

What is now striking about many of the political movements we have studied is not so much their relationship to class but their essential maleness. Masculinity is as much a part of gender history as femininity. The paradox of radical culture was that it was imbued with an egalitarian ethos (including at times sexual egalitarianism) and yet in practice it restricted female participation. Radicals often employed the language of sexual equality while failing to transcend the masculine orientation of their movement.[22] Incorporating gender into our analysis therefore provides for a different kind of narrative from that based on class or the constitution. We need to re-conceive the story of popular politics in terms of contestations of gender roles. The long-term consequence of this was that women frequently found themselves excluded from a male dominated labour movement that professed to believe in female equality.[23]

SOCIALISM

At its crudest, the old analysis employed English working-class experience as a model of proletarianisation where industrial capitalism generated alienation and class consciousness leading to the emergence of socialism in the later nineteenth century. Radicalism and liberalism were apparently elbowed aside by a modern ideology that made sense of working-class exploitation. Yet English socialism was also seen by left-wing historians as unsatisfactory, travelling light on theory unlike its continental counterparts. In practice, socialism was strangled by labourism which rarely strayed beyond the boundaries of parliamentary democracy. Although the language of class became dominant in the later nineteenth century, working-class culture was distinctive for its fatalism and pragmatism. A dislike of 'Them' (the employing classes) was accompanied by a belief that the system could not be changed.[24] Marxian socialism never had a chance in a culture dominated by fish and chips and the cloth cap. Late Victorian socialists frequently found themselves at odds with a popular culture which they could not identify with.[25] Robert Roberts recalls how in Edwardian Salford

> Marxist 'ranters'... who paid fleeting visits to our street end insisted that we, the proletariat, stood locked in titanic struggle with some wicked master class. We were battling, they told us (from a vinegar barrel, borrowed from our corner shop) to cast off our chains and win a whole world. Most people passed by; a few stood to listen, but not for long: the problems of the 'proletariat', they felt, had little to do with them.[26]

Given that socialism has received a lot of attention from historians, it is worth remembering that it was a minority tradition in the nineteenth century, less important than traditional radicalism. However, by the end of the century, increasing numbers of workers were identifying themselves with the doctrine. To what extent was socialism a departure in radical culture?

'Socialism' had several meanings during the century. Up to the 1850s, it was primarily associated with the ideas of Robert Owen and signified a non-revolutionary, communitarian critique of capitalism. Owenism was often considered unrespectable because it was secularist and its critique of marriage created a gulf between Owen and other radicals. Gregory Claeys has shown that Owenism was also derived from the radical tradition. It shared radicalism's desire to extend popular sovereignty and its belief that freedom could best be maintained through small-scale communities.[27] Like radicalism, it was inspired by puritanism in the form of quakerism with its spirit of equality. However, its intentions went beyond the scope of traditional radicalism. It attempted to transcend government (what Claeys calls 'anti-politics') because the state was not capable of resolving the complex questions posed by the machine age. It was therefore resistant to the radical analysis which blamed social evils on taxation and 'Old Corruption'. Instead, it countered the individualism of modern society with support for collectivism based on egalitarian communities. Owen moved beyond moral economy/just price arguments to locate exploitation in the control of machinery.[28] The Owenite tradition declined in the 1850s but its legacy was threefold. It developed the land issue as a radical cause. It inspired the co-operative movement which in the mid-Victorian period provided another meeting point between middle-class liberalism and radicalism. But, most important of all, it generated the idea of the 'social' and hence of 'social reform', challenging traditional radicals to think in terms of society rather than the individual.[29]

In the 1840s, a new definition of socialism emerged which was based on revolutionary transformation. By the mid-Victorian period, the revolutionary, Marxist form of socialism was advocated by, among other people, Marx himself in the International Working Men's Association and other radical clubs in London. Many socialists saw themselves as building on the radical analysis of the Chartist Bronterre O'Brien, particularly in the area of land nationalisation. The Soho O'Brienites and the Manhood Suffrage League formed a link between Chartism and late Victorian socialism, another example of radical continuity.[30] True to their Chartist principles, many of them were active in the Reform League which agitated for the expansion of the franchise in the 1860s and were partially rewarded with the 1867 Reform Act.

The emergence of socialism in the 1880s and 1890s is usually seen as the product of a new class consciousness. The capitalist economy had reached maturity leading to the formation of an organised labour movement, evident in the New Unionism of the unskilled. The Social Democratic Federation (SDF) which became a socialist organisation in 1884 advocated revolution and nationalisation. Led by Henry Hyndman, a former Tory businessman, the SDF included amongst its members the artist and poet William Morris who later formed a break-away group, the Socialist League. The moderate Fabian Society (founded in 1884) argued for an extreme form of liberalism based on state intervention. Both the SDF and the Fabians are usually considered departures from the forms of radicalism discussed in Chapter Five. In some ways they were, but it is significant that both movements were influenced by old radicalism, believing in the importance of purely political reform. The Fabians retained the traditional radical distinction between the industrious and the unproductive, although they were not hostile to the state.[31] The SDF began life as the Democratic Federation in 1881, essentially a Chartist organisation. Many early supporters had been followers of Bronterre O'Brien and shared his emphasis on political solutions to social evils. The Democratic Federation was committed to a broadly Chartist package of democracy and land nationalisation. Although the Marxist notion of taking over the means of production and expropriating the capitalists had become widespread by the mid-1880s, the SDF maintained its

O'Brienite political strategy.[32] Thus the organisation was in the fore-front of political groups advocating democracy at all levels of society.[33] The new socialism was as much a continuation of traditional radicalism as a new departure.

By the end of the century, there was a third strain of socialism. Ethical socialism was not based on a determinist or Marxist model; rather, it was derived from a moral and religious critique of capitalism, embodied in the nonconformist values of the Independent Labour Party.[34] In contrast to the scientific socialism of the SDF, capitalism was simply denounced as immoral and inefficient. The first Labour MPs derived their inspiration not from Marx but from the Bible and John Bunyan as well as the works of Dickens, Ruskin and Carlyle.[35] It is now a commonplace that the Labour Party owes more to Methodism than to Marxism. Significantly, the Independent Labour Party held its first conference in a disused chapel in Bradford in 1893. The ethos of the Labour Party when it emerged in 1900 as the Labour Representation Committee came from an inward looking defence of the rights of labour. The culture of labourism privileged the views of the trade union movement and was often concerned with short-term goals.

A fourth definition of socialism began to emerge after mid-century when the term came to be associated with state intervention. Thus it is not surprising that Labour supporters found it easy to collaborate with Liberal progressives, especially in the expanding world of local govern-ment in the 1890s.[36] Liberals increasingly came to stress public ownership at the municipal level. By turn, Labour supporters such as Ramsay MacDonald spoke in terms of enhancing the community rather than practising class warfare.

However, it would be a mistake to assume that socialism was simply a continuation of old radicalism in a new guise. For many of its adher-ents socialism meant the future, a new society based on equality and modernity.[37] The Owenite belief in a 'New Moral World' was echoed in the visionary nature of late Victorian socialism. For William Morris' generation, radicalism and liberalism were limited in their ability to generate effective social change and a new approach was needed for tackling social problems. The gulf between the old radi-calism and socialism was evident in a debate between Hyndman and the radical Charles Bradlaugh in 1884. Bradlaugh defined the differ-ence between their positions in this way:

> we both recognise many social evils. He (Hyndman) wants the State to remedy them, I want the individuals to remedy them.[38]

Although socialism was always on the periphery in radical politics (at least up to 1900), it exerted an influence far beyond its small number of devotees. In the old analysis, popular radicalism tended to be seen as an inferior form of socialism. What is now clear is how robust old radicalism was, such that even socialism was shaped by it.

Yet there is another paradox about English socialism. Hyndman claimed to believe in international socialism. The socialist analysis saw the class struggle in international terms and therefore disdained jingoism. Yet Hyndman hated foreigners and was determined to prove that socialism was an authentic English doctrine as a defence against the charge that Marxian socialism was foreign (and therefore suspect).[39] Whilst Hyndman was a one-off, socialism has often been mediated by radical patriotism, evident in Robert Blatchford's *Merrie England* (1894). We must therefore consider how the nation helped construct political identity.

7　The nation and politics I
Patriotism

BRINGING THE NATION BACK IN

It was not unusual amongst the Victorian working class to believe that 'an Englishman is as good as three Frenchmen (or any foreigners); that in fighting he could "lick" them; in the peaceful contests of labour "work their heads off"'.[1] This chapter and the next consider the role of national identity in popular politics. It was through the language of patriotism and the nation that political struggles were often played out. Defining the different views of the nation is therefore central to an understanding of popular politics. The nation is a relatively new subject for modern British historians. Until recently, workers were believed to have only a class identity rather than a national one and left-wing historians (considering themselves heirs to a tradition of internationalism dating back to Paine) have felt uncomfortable discussing it. Patriotism and popular imperialism were considered irrational emotions. Moreover, for historians in general, nationalism was something that happened elsewhere. English or British nationalism was a non-subject despite the fact that the iconography of the nation has pervaded British life and institutions over the last two centuries.

The political right (which believes itself to have a monopoly on nationhood) considers nationalism a universal and unchanging feeling shared by all. However, it has been clear to historians for a long time that the nation state and hence nationalism was and is historically specific. Nationalism in its modern sense really only emerged in the later eighteenth century, signalled by the American and French revolutions. Furthermore, modern nationalism came to include a definition of national identity based on ethnicity and language, an association that was only forged in the nineteenth century.[2] Modern commentators have drawn attention to the artificial nature of nationalism. In the words of Benedict Anderson, nations are 'imagined communities', a form of identity that has to be constructed and which should therefore have the status of a powerful form of mythology.[3] The nation itself does not exist. It can only be constructed through the work of politicians, intellectuals and institutions, appropriating popular concerns. British historians locate this, for example, in what has been termed the 'invention of tradition'. They reveal how many of the traditional emblems of Englishness (such as the Changing of the Guard) are in fact only a century old and were invented to justify the existence of the British elite which felt itself to be under threat in the later nineteenth century.[4]

Nationalism should be distinguished from patriotism. Patriotism describes the broad, unstructured affections for a particular locality or homeland. The chief characteristic of nationalism is that it transforms these raw, untutored emotions into a coherent political ideology based on citizenship, language and ethnicity.[5] This chapter however, employs the two terms interchangeably, mainly because the term 'patriotism' was so frequently used in the period under discussion.

Nationalism in a British context is complicated by the fact that British history is the story of four nations.[6] Englishness has competed with the national identities of Scotland, Ireland and Wales as well as with a generalised Britishness from the later eighteenth century onwards. However, the construction of nationalism required the existence of an 'other' against which national identity could be defined.[7] This 'other' was often located in France or, sometimes, in Russia or Turkey and, closer to home, in Ireland. The Catholicism of other countries helped define the essentially Protestant nature of Britain. The Empire and Britain's relationship to non-white peoples also determined the construction of British nationhood. National identity therefore is not an ongoing emotion; rather, it is contingent on specific events and based on relationships with other nations. It is also possible to have several different national identities at the same time (to be English as well as British).

In the 1970s, those historians of popular politics who did tackle the question of national identity attempted to undermine the whole notion of a patriotic proletariat. Henry Pelling and Richard Price both criticised the idea that imperialism established deep roots amongst the late Victorian working class. Price in particular focused on the pro-Boer resistance to the Boer War and located jingoism primarily amongst the lower middle class, especially clerks.[8] Similarly, Hugh Cunningham's study of the Volunteer force found that 'patriotism was of relatively minor importance' in accounting for its popularity.[9] Set up in 1859 after an invasion scare, the Volunteers drew extensively on working-class support and were a symbol of class harmony following the turmoil of the Chartist period. Cunningham's study demonstrated that enlistment in the Volunteers was prompted as much by a desire for the recreational facilities involved and for upward social mobility as by nationalism. However, there were other accounts that pointed to the centrality of patriotism amongst the working class. Gareth Stedman Jones' work on late Victorian London established that music hall jingoism was integral to a reconstructed popular culture that emerged after the demise of Chartism. He dubbed this the 'culture of consolation' because it was based on pleasure not politics, on resignation to the fact that capitalism could not be overturned.[10] Patriotism provided the lowest common denominator in the cheap and cheerful world of the music hall, playing to an apathetic working class. Alternatively, E.P. Thompson's evocation of the 'freeborn Englishman' in the 1960s had suggested a patriotic tradition that stood in opposition to jingoism.[11]

During the 1980s, patriotism, having been on the fringes of historical inquiry, moved to centre stage. The survival of the United Kingdom seemed in doubt given the enduring strength of nationalist sentiment in Scotland, Wales and (especially) Northern Ireland. At the same time, Britain's relationship with Europe remained a continuing source of division amongst politicians. In Eastern Europe, nationalism re-emerged in a dynamic form in 1989 and afterwards. All of this made national identity an object of fascination and the historical literature on nationalism expanded dramatically. British historians were also propelled towards the nation as a subject in order to understand popular support for the Conservative Party under the flag-waving leadership of Margaret Thatcher and the jingoism evident during the Falklands conflict of 1982. This produced not only an investigation of the institutions and culture that bolstered conservatism but also a literature on the construction of both English and British nationalism.[12] In order to make sense of the nation as a category in popular politics, we must therefore examine how it was appropriated by both radicals and conservatives.

RADICAL PATRIOTISM

Modern scholarship in this area really began with a path-breaking article by Hugh Cunningham which showed that patriotism was not the sole preserve of the right.[13] During the eighteenth century and for most of the nineteenth patriotism constituted the basic ideology of radicalism and a language of opposition through which elites could be attacked. Elites were represented as selfish and devoid of national feeling whereas radicals could claim a nobility of spirit through their concern for the good of the country. Other historians such as Kathleen Wilson have confirmed this. Patriotism was evident in the cult of Admiral Vernon who defeated the Spanish at Porto Bello in 1739. His credentials as a critic of the Walpole administration made him the focus for anti-government feeling that linked libertarianism with support for overseas expansion.[14] When the Tory Dr Johnson complained that 'patriotism is the last refuge of a scoundrel', he was in fact attacking radicalism. The culture of eighteenth-century radical patriotism took diverse forms including anti-Catholicism, imperialism and hostility to foreigners. The elite in turn found it difficult to employ the language of patriotism because it was imbued with assumptions about citizens' rights. Hence supporters of the British government during the French Revolutionary period were known as Loyalists rather than as Patriots.[15] Cunningham argued that this language of selfless patriotism did not die away with the nineteenth century but remained the language of radicalism right through to the 1870s when Benjamin Disraeli began to annex patriotism for the Conservative Party. In other words, patriotism underpinned the continuity of radical thought described in Chapter Five. The nation was therefore a key constituent of popular ideology with important links to constitutionalism. Loyalism was matched by the radical insistence on the duty of a patriot and freeborn Englishman to oppose the government. Patriotism did not exclude class but it wove in and out of the radical mindset, generating support and identifying the 'other' in 'Old Corruption'. It had an integrative function.

English nationalism was matched by an increasing sense of what it was to be British. Linda Colley's *Britons* (1992) described the way in which a distinctively British identity was created. Conscious of the many forms of conflict in the national culture (core/periphery, Anglican/nonconformist), she insisted that we also need to think about the ways in which the nation provided the basis for consensus. A British identity slowly emerged in the wake of the Act of Union with Scotland in 1707 but gathered pace after the suppression of the Jacobite rebellion in 1745. The experience of warfare in the late eighteenth and early nineteenth centuries combined with an invigorated Protestantism to bind subjects together. The charisma of leaders such as both Pitts and the Duke of Wellington forged a national identity that was heroic but also defensive. In politics, the nation was something that was invoked on all sides. For example, John Bull became an important British emblem, standing for stoicism and common sense.

Both radicals and conservatives claimed him as their own. The radical John Bull valued fairness and equality. The conservative John Bull stood for fiscal rectitude. In the midst of the Queen Caroline affair, radicals, Whigs and Tories all claimed his support.[16] The British identity traced by Colley was complete by the 1830s but it was contested by the growth of Irish nationalism (see p. 86). Moreover, in the later nineteenth century, it co-existed with an identity based on militiant Englishness in which 'England' came to stand for the whole of Britain.[17]

Our understanding of patriotism is clouded by an approach derived from the Edwardian era when liberal intellectuals found themselves assailed by popular support for jingoism.[18] Patriotism since then has been associated with chauvinistic bombast. However, as Miles Taylor has argued, if we are to comprehend Victorian patriotism, then we must encounter it on its own terms and not through the eyes of Edwardian intellectuals or through the assumptions of the present day.[19] Seeking out patriotism in this way counters the view that it is something that is unchanging, an essential part of the core being of every Briton. There were in fact several patriotisms derived from different understandings of the nation, the Empire and race. I am concerned here to delineate the range of core concerns that characterised the radical patriotic imagination.

Wherever one looks, the language of patriotism pervaded radical culture, from William Cobbett's defence of the values of English yeomen in the years after Waterloo to Henry Hyndman's *England for All* (1881), the work of a cricket-loving, foreigner-hating socialist. In the 1840s the radical paper in Brighton was the *Brighton Patriot*. James Wheeler, the Manchester radical, who was wounded at Peterloo, took pride in the fact that he was arrested no less than eighteen times for his 'patriotic conduct'.[20] Radical patriotism defined itself through the exclusion of the 'other', particularly the French. Gallophobia was an integral part of political culture, both radical and conservative. Indeed, Gerald Newman suggests that the French Revolution damaged radicalism because it was unable to deploy its customary anti-French vocabulary.[21] France up to that time had been a byword for poverty and for effete and despotic values amongst its elite. The coming of Napoleon rescued radicalism, providing it with the opportunity to oppose tyranny once more. The issue of foreign despotism accounts for the continuing anti-Russian tradition that lasted through the century. Against this, nineteenth-century radicals tended to view the United States of America as a treasure trove of Anglo-Saxon radical values (although blighted by the survival of slavery up to 1865).

Love of country did not preclude a sympathy for nationalist causes elsewhere. Radicalism developed an abiding culture of internationalism which Margot Finn suggests was actually founded on nationalism itself.[22] From the 1840s to the 1860s (years of nationalist struggles throughout Europe), patriots recognised their counterparts in other countries and eagerly organised committees to support them. Lord Palmerston's support for nationalism abroad made him the unlikely hero of working-class politicians and eased relations between parliamentary Radicals and Whigs in the 1850s.[23] Britain became a refuge for political exiles (most famously, Karl Marx) whilst nationalist figures such as the Italian Mazzini and the Hungarian Kossuth became leading celebrities. The visit of Garibaldi in 1864 provided the inspiration for the Reform League whose demand for the extension of the suffrage bore fruit in the Reform Act of 1867. Cobdenite Free Trade provided a vehicle for co-operation between middle- and working-class radicals and for an accommodation between the claims of class and nation. The identification with freedom struggles abroad was based on a liberal and pacific view of the nation (as opposed to an imperialist view). Britain's moral mission was to promote international justice and understanding. A nation that had the courage to abolish slavery and the slave trade had the potential to introduce social harmony both at home and abroad. The radical view of foreign policy therefore cannot be divorced from its approach to home affairs. Each was part of a broader patriotic vision.

There were of course other forms of nationalism apart from English nationalism. The Irish in England are sometimes seen as a distinctive group in Victorian society, their national identity and Catholicism resented in a Protestant country. They were a people apart, an apparently divisive force in working-class politics. Daniel O'Connell, the great Irish leader and promoter of Catholic Emancipation, insisted that Irish nationalism should be kept separate from English radicalism. In Liverpool and Manchester, relations between O'Connellites and English radicals could be actively hostile. Although many of the great radical leaders such as John Doherty, Feargus O'Connor and Bronterre O'Brien were Irish, J.H. Treble has argued that Irish immigrants remained aloof from radicalism and Chartism until 1848. Dorothy Thompson, however, disputes this arguing that there was a significant Irish presence in Chartism which went beyond the leadership. It is not coincidental that towns such as Barnsley, Bradford and Ashton which enjoyed a high incidence of Chartist activity also had substantial Irish populations. Not for nothing was the Chartist *Northern Star* named after the newspaper of the United Irishmen in the 1790s.[24]

Indeed, looking across the period under discussion, the Irish issue continually intersected with English radicalism, demonstrating the complex nature of political identity.[25] William Cobbett was deeply concerned about the poverty of the Irish and, like other radicals, feared that authoritarian rule in Ireland would translate into authoritarianism in England. Henry Hunt ensured that the radical mass platform included Catholic Emancipation and appealed to Irish immigrants. All authorities agree that the Irish played an important part in the last phase of Chartism in 1848. Ethnic tensions were to some extent buried by a general radical sympathy for the Irish cause. A delegation of Irish Confederates attended the Kennington Common demonstration on 10 April 1848. Later that year, the Chartist Ernest Jones proclaimed to a crowd that 'Only preparation – only organisation is wanted, and the Green Flag shall float over Downing Street, and St Stephen's'.[26] The subsequent suspension of *habeas corpus* in Ireland triggered mass meetings in Birmingham, Bolton, Manchester and Liverpool. John Belchem suggests that the upsurge in ultra-Protestantism and anti-Irish riots that characterised the mid-Victorian period had their roots in 1848, contributing to the stereotype of the Irish as disloyal and prone to rebellion. Later, the outrage over Fenian activities in 1867 generated anti-Irish fervour. However, radical sympathies with the Irish continued. The Democratic Federation (later the SDF) was partly established in 1881 as an organisation to combat an Irish Coercion Bill. Support for changing Britain's constitutional links with Ireland (even if it often stopped short of outright nationalism) was another dimension to the continuity of radicalism described in Chapter Five.

Radicals were frequently ambivalent about the British Empire, rarely demanding its break-up because, at its best, it provided for the spread of citizenship across the globe. However, radicals frequently complained about the expense of imperialism and the way in which it burdened those who paid taxes either directly or indirectly. They disliked the grandeur of Empire, especially when it was seen as the plaything of the aristocracy. In the 1890s, this was identified as the mentality of the 'Little Englander' who was both a patriot and opposed to most forms of British intervention abroad.[27] These were the people that A.J.P. Taylor termed 'the trouble makers', the radicals who opposed the Crimean and Boer Wars.[28] This tradition was an outgrowth of the nonconformist conscience. During episodes such as the Bulgarian agitation of 1876, nonconformists displayed a remarkable sympathy for countries portrayed at the time as Britain's enemies. Radicals were trouble makers because they believed that the foreign policy elite had forgotten its duty to stand for justice between nations.

Religion was central to radical patriotism. Anglicans and nonconformists shared a Protestant heritage, derived from such works as Foxe's *Book of Martyrs* (1563), which suggested that England was an elect nation enjoying a special relationship with God, comparable to that enjoyed by the Hebrews in the Bible.[29] This was a particular feature of evangelical thought which defined freedom in terms of Protestantism. Belief in the Protestant nation was both a unifying and divisive force.[30] Catholicism, despite emancipation in 1829, was usually seen as beyond the pale as was Judaism.

Patriotism therefore cannot be divorced from the issue of ethnicity and indeed of race. The language of the freeborn Englishman was based on universal rights and the alleged superiority of Protestant Anglo-Saxon values. For example, the campaign to abolish slavery was derived from a view of black slaves as part of a universal brotherhood. However, from the mid-Victorian period onwards, the issue of white supremacy gained ground, evident particularly in the campaign over Governor Eyre and his treatment of the rebellion at Morant Bay in Jamaica in 1865.[31] The debate on Eyre coincided with the revival of the issue of parliamentary reform. The Reform Act of 1867 was premised on competing forms of citizenship. An extended franchise was granted to the British whereas the rights of those in the colonies were denied.[32]

This last example speaks to an agenda that is beginning to emerge amongst historians. Understanding British history in purely domestic terms is proving unsatisfactory because it ignores the fact that Britain in this period was steadily gaining control of one third of the earth's surface. Increasing attention is currently being devoted to the implications of this for all aspects of British life. Our understanding of the links between radicalism and Empire is still in its infancy. Much of radical culture at the end of the day was concerned with purely local or domestic matters. Ethnic conflicts usually revolved around English, Welsh, Scottish and Irish identities rather than the Empire. However, large numbers of labourers worked in industries that were tied to foreign and imperial markets. We have much to learn about how radicals measured their own patriotism and demands for citizenship against those of people abroad. There was also a black presence in popular radicalism. Robert Wedderburn, the follower of the proto-socialist Thomas Spence, was the son of a Jamaican slave. William Cuffay the Chartist was also black. The second half of the century saw a widespread attempt to put race on an allegedly scientific basis. Social Darwinism at the end of the century was based on a concern to maintain the fitness of the Anglo-Saxon race. At a popular level, this belief in white supremacy fed into the cult of imperialism in the late Victorian period.

The Englishness promulgated by radicals drew on the importance of national character. From the eighteenth century onwards, this was based on a view of Englishness that emphasised sincerity as opposed to the duplicity of the aristocracy.[33] Englishness came to mean plain speaking, a love of basic pleasures such as roast beef and beer and a dislike of unnecessary ornamentation. 'Character' in itself was a key word for the Victorians. The radical patriot was a person distinguished by an attachment to liberty and a hatred of despotism and centralisation. Much radical activity can be seen as an attempt to defend these values. Although these were often imagined in masculine terms (the values of John Bull), the nation was usually figured as a woman. Britannia first appeared on coins in 1665 and was identified with religious and political liberty, naval supremacy and imperialism.[34] Women are often used in art and culture not as representations of themselves as human beings but as allegories. They are intended as propaganda or symbols for experience: hence Britannia or Marianne (in France). As we saw in the Queen Caroline case, women could be symbolically central to the radical patriotic imagination, despite the chauvinism frequently on display.

The revival of interest in the nation poses the question of whether radicalism should be re-conceived as a set of nationalist movements comparable to other nationalist movements around the world in the same period. Such a view would be an exaggeration. Radicals were not trying to establish a new state with its own territorial integrity as happened, for example, in the Italian Risorgimento. Radicalism should instead be seen as an attempt to provide an alternative vision of the nation based on the values of liberty and citizenship.

Radical patriotism did not decline in the later nineteenth century. From Hyndman through to George Orwell and on to Michael Foot, patriotism and a belief in the essential virtues of Englishness provided the glue which held radicalism together, despite its commitment to internationalism. However, the nation was not the sole preserve of radicals. Throughout the century, it was appropriated in increasingly successful ways by the Conservative Party.

8   The nation and politics II
Popular conservatism

Whilst historians have been uncomfortable with the idea of the nation in popular politics, they have been positively embarrassed by popular conservatism. Whether defined as support for the Conservative Party or as a basic sympathy with British institutions and the market economy, popular conservatism presents a dimension of politics that historians have often opted to ignore. Even right-wing historians have not chosen to extol the virtues of the bloody-minded, tub-thumping, beer-barrel jingoism that characterised Toryism in the later Victorian years. However, as recounted in Chapter Two, continued working-class support for Margaret Thatcher in the 1980s meant that popular conservatism could no longer be ignored and its roots demanded explanation. Apart from anything else, the continuing history and success of popular conservatism provides one explanation for the failure of working-class radical organisations.

Like radicalism and liberalism, popular conservatism appropriated the themes of the nation and the constitution. From the 1870s onwards, the Conservative Party struggled to make the nation its own and rooted itself in a militant Englishness. Benjamin Disraeli portrayed the Liberals as unpatriotic, the party of special interest groups and of the periphery of the British Isles. He denied that the working classes entertained radical beliefs:

> They repudiate cosmopolitan principles. They adhere to national principles.[1]

As early as 1858, the liberal John Bright felt he had to complain to an audience about this supposed concern with national principles:

> How, indeed, can I, any more than any of you be un-English and anti-national? Was I not born upon the same soil? Do I not come of the same English stock? . . . Then how shall men dare to say to one

of his countrymen, because he happens to hold a different opinion on questions of great public policy that therefore he is un-English, and is to be condemned as anti-national?[2]

The nation provides a key to understanding popular conservatism.

Given the numerous periods of economic depression and the emergence of class politics, popular conservatism may surprise us. Indeed, it is often discussed as a form of aberrant or deviant political behaviour. But the enduring history of popular conservatism makes sense if we view it through the lens of cultural history. Conservatism as a political force has relied heavily on the symbolic and been unafraid to appeal to the irrational. At a popular level, it was based on popular instincts and what it constructed as common sense rather than any political programme.

Popular conservatism, however, was not confined to the second half of the century (although this is the period that has received the most research). In the 1790s, the Church and King Mob militantly opposed the claims of radicalism and harassed anyone who dared oppose the government. This cohered into popular Loyalism, based around the significantly named Pitt clubs. In the decade after 1815, Loyalism took as its task the defence of the constitution against the mass platform constructed by radicals. Although this did not lead to any enduring organisations, the existence of Loyalism suggested that the Tory government of Lord Liverpool could command considerable popular support. This did not transform the essentially aristocratic nature of conservatism. In the 1830s, *Blackwood's Edinburgh Magazine* suggested an alliance between the Tory Party and the working class to counter middle-class support for the Whigs.[3] The belief that both ends could be pitted against the middle provided the basis for a culture of popular conservatism. The 1830s witnessed the emergence of a strain of radical Toryism, personified by such figures as the 'Factory King' Richard Oastler. Divorced from the philosophy of Sir Robert Peel and much of the Conservative Party in Parliament, radical Toryism became the ideology of paternalism. It criticised the new industrial order, identified with the Whigs, because it had overturned traditional patterns of obligation between rich and poor. The decade also marked the growth of local Conservative organisations with a popular base. Some of these had originated during the French Revolution as a riposte to the growth of Jacobin societies. Local Conservative societies aimed directly at the working classes were formed in Lancashire and the West Riding of Yorkshire. By 1836 there were one hundred societies.[4] The purpose of these organisations was to oppose reform. The rules of the Leeds Conservative Operative Society, founded in 1835, stated:

> We reverence the king and all in authority, and pay due deference and respect to all who are in high stations ... because we believe that the different degrees and orders in society are so closely united and interwoven with each other that, when we exalt them, we raise ourselves; as, should we depress them, we proportionately lower ourselves. While we maintain their rights, we secure our own, and while we defend their privileges, we increase our own.[5]

Such was the dislike of centralisation that these organisations had very little to do with the parliamentary party. They were mainly active in voter registration, particularly amongst shopkeepers. Their success in appealing to the working class remains unclear from current research. This network of Conservative associations was only broken by the split within the party over the repeal of the Corn Laws in 1846.

A new network of Conservative organisations began in 1863 with the formation of the Conservative Registration Association (which became a formal part of the Conservative political machine three years later). The National Union of Conservative and Constitutional Associations was established in 1867 and Conservative Central Office in 1870. The key to these developments was the expansion of the suffrage in 1867, creating a mass electorate which had to be organised. Liberal legislation in 1883 restricted the use of professional political agents which led to the creation that year of the Primrose League whose purpose was to provide voluntary workers for the party.[6] The 1870s witnessed a considerable expansion in popular conservatism, partly through better party organisation and some popular resistance to Gladstone's Liberal administration (1868–74) but also because the party promoted a populist version of the nation. The Conservatives in the election of 1874 made great gains in Lancashire where they traded on being the Protestant party and hence appealed to workers who disliked the presence of Irish immigrants. Significantly, when Disraeli had visited Manchester in 1872 to give one of his speeches that appealed for working-class support, he was welcomed by a network of local Orange lodges and Conservative associations. He was also applauded in Manchester as the author of *Sybil*, his novel of 1845 which condemned the division of England into the 'Two Nations' of rich and poor. Disraeli was therefore able to appropriate many of the themes of social reform normally associated with the Liberals. The mid-Victorian Conservative Party was able to appeal to a popular culture in Lancashire and surrounding areas that combined a populist celebration of working-class lifestyles with a vigorous deference to social superiors, evident in the factory paternalism of northern industrial towns. Thus in 1858, nine hundred workers marched through Stalybridge with 'Long life to our employers' and 'Britannia rules the waves' on their banners.[7] Robert Roberts' memoirs of his youth in Salford at the beginning of the twentieth century also recall a deferential culture of employer-paternalism:

> Many were genuinely grateful to an employer for being kind enough to use their services at all. Voting Conservative, they felt at one with him. It was their belief, expressed at election times, that the middle and upper classes with their better intelligence and education had a natural right to think and act on behalf of the rest.[8]

However, the genius of later Victorian conservatism was its ability to expand its appeal to suburban, middle-class ratepayers ('Villa Toryism'). In the election of 1885, following the subdivision of borough constituencies, the Conservatives actually managed to obtain a majority of English boroughs, showing that their appeal was no longer restricted to the counties. The advent of mass democracy between 1867 and 1885 transformed the Conservatives from an aristocratic party into an organisation that could appeal to all classes. Middle-class voters increasingly took fright at Liberal reforms, especially after Gladstone adopted Irish Home Rule in 1886. From 1886 through to 1906, the Conservatives enjoyed a twenty-year dominance in politics (with the exception of 1892 to 1895). This hegemony may have been more apparent than real. It was dependent on low turnouts and the disarray of the opposition rather than on the popularity of the party although its association with imperialism did it no harm. E.H.H. Green argues that the reason that the Conservatives turned to tariff reform in the early twentieth century was that they needed an issue with which to appeal to an enlarged electorate on which they could not rely. Their failure to win the elections of 1910 with this stance combined with the rise of Labour to bring the Conservatives close to destruction. It was only the realignment of politics during the First World War that saved the party.[9]

Popular conservatism is often viewed as a form of deviancy within a modern class society. Marx and Engels associated it with the *lumpenproletariat* arguing that its conditions of life prepared the '"dangerous class", the social scum, that passively rotting mass thrown off by the lowest layers of old society . . . for the part of a bribed tool of reactionary intrigue'.[10] However, Patrick Joyce's research on the second half of the century suggests that conservatism could be found in all parts of the working classes.[11] Three explanations are usually given for popular conservatism: deference, populism and support for imperialism. From the French Revolution onwards, Conservatives adhered to an ideology of paternalism and warned that British institutions were under threat. The pamphlets of Hannah More in the 1790s urged respect for those in authority. Rural England in particular was characterised by the widespread culture of deference to the aristocracy. Joyce showed how this was transferred to employers in northern industrial towns after mid-century.[12] Support for the Conservative Party therefore carried associations of status and prestige because it was the party of the aristocracy. Although bound up with the class system, the appeal of popular conservatism could be oddly classless. It spoke the language of chivalry and romanticism, a yearning for a time long gone, usually pre-industrial, rural or even feudal. The culture of conservatism transcended class in favour of the nation. It was grounded in a view of society as based on community rather than organised around atomised individuals. This view of society as an organism is often associated with Edmund Burke, the conservative philosopher whose 'Tree of State' was emblazoned on banners in Lancashire Tory demonstrations in 1877–78.[13]

The Conservative Party was militantly populist, taking the side of popular culture against middle-class busy-bodies who wanted to reform it. Although paternalist, conservatism was not patronising. Frequently, Conservatives spoke the same language as Radicals with their emphasis on the constitution in danger and concern for the welfare of the common people and of the nation. Here, the values of conservatism blended with late Victorian mass culture, particularly the music hall. Although rarely political, the cheap patriotism and sentimental evocation of working-class life in the music hall echoed the popular approach of the Conservative Party. Gladstone's Licensing Act of 1872 allowed the Conservative Party to pose as the defenders of the working man's right to drink. Robert Roberts recalled that Salford publicans 'were Tories almost to a man and the party's self-appointed agents'.[14] Similarly, Toryism was associated with the world of sport, particularly the race course. What united aristocrat and worker was therefore not just paternalism but pleasure, a headlong celebration of the joys of life. The Primrose League, outside of elections, was mainly a social club. The League tended to ignore detailed political issues and concentrated on key themes or principles such as defence of the Empire and the Church of England. Indeed, it was technically not part of the Conservative Party at all. This was the secret of its success because it was able to present the Conservatives as the non-political

political party. Its appeal was based on vagueness and a belief that politics should be conducted through common sense rather than ideological programmes. Radicals who emphasised politics were bores.[15]

Conservative support for the monarchy, the Empire and the Church provided a form of constitutionalism that easily matched that of radicalism. Conservatives saw themselves as custodians of the nation and characterised everyone else as selfish cliques who would betray the nation's interests. They maintained that they had tradition on their side; hence, the mediaevalism of their rhetoric and their frequent invocations of the feudal order as a time of lost paternalism. However, this approach did not exclude the importance of self help; Conservative clubs sometimes launched friendly societies. Nor did it prevent the Conservative Party becoming a party of social reform. Late Victorian Tories frequently highlighted the issue of working-class housing. The Primrose League was particularly effective in its recruitment of women. As we have seen, radical movements frequently relegated women to the home but the gender politics of the League found room for women (known as Primrose Dames). Women became central to the organisation of the movement and hence of the Conservative Party, working side by side with men.[16] Thus it is not surprising that some parts of the Conservative Party became increasingly sympathetic to the issue of female suffrage and that the Conservatives after 1918 were extremely successful in their appeal to women voters.

Imperialism did not evoke much interest in the first half of the century. However, from the 1860s, justifications for Empire became more marked. There were different kinds of imperialism based on free trade, the advance of missionary activity or the extension of Anglo-Saxon values. Empire was often associated with heroism or Christian martyrdom, evident in the cult of General Sir Henry Havelock who died during the Indian Mutiny in 1857. Through a detailed reading of popular newspapers, Virginia Berridge has pointed to a marked increase in interest and concern for the Empire during the 1870s and 1880s.[17] The working class was bombarded with images of imperialism.[18] Music hall culture in particular extolled the virtues of the Empire. In 1878, the music hall artiste, the Great MacDermott, introduced a new word into the language at a time when Britain seemed close to war with Russia over the Eastern Question:

We don't want to fight, but by jingo if we do,
We got the guns, we've got the men, we've got the money too.

By and large, peacetime helped the Liberals whilst war or the prospect of war unleashed a tide of what we now call 'jingoism'.

Popular conservatism appealed to a culture that enjoyed military spectacle, either in the form of demonstrations by the Volunteer force or patriotic displays in the theatre or circus. The figure of the 'jack tar' (the ordinary naval seaman) was an enduring heroic figure on the stage. By the last decade of the nineteenth century, there was a greater concentration on presenting nationalist or imperialist messages to young people, a process that flourished in the Edwardian era. It was the genius of the Conservative Party that it associated itself with this dimension of popular culture. Disraeli told his supporters in 1872 that 'the people of England, and especially the working classes of England, are proud of belonging to an imperial country, and are resolved to maintain if they can, their Empire'.[19]

However, not only were the Conservatives linked to Empire, they were also the party of the monarchy. David Cannadine has argued that the monarchy was remarkably unpopular throughout the century. The funerals of Wellington and Nelson produced far more interest than the funerals or weddings of royalty which he puts down to the ineptness of royal ceremonial. A more professional approach to ceremonial was responsible for the seachange in popular attitudes in the late Victorian period. The reconstruction of central London as an imperial city helped but it was the Jubilees of 1887 and 1897 during the heyday of invented tradition that really cemented the link between the royal family and the people, an association that persists today.[20] It also saw off the republican movement that had briefly flourished in the mid-Victorian period.[21] However, there was always a groundswell of enthusiasm for the monarchy throughout the century evident at the beginning of the period under discussion in the support for George III.[22] But the monarchy was not necessarily a Conservative icon. Radicals often began meetings with a toast to the monarch and there was a popular idea that the monarch (particularly Victoria) was sympathetic to the people but was kept back from them by a government conspiracy. Disraeli's skill consisted in appropriating the monarchy for the Conservative Party at a time when royal celebrations were on the increase. Thus by the late Victorian period, a set of institutions and forms of rhetoric were in place that positioned the Conservatives as the party of Empire, monarchy and constitution and more profoundly as the natural party of government. This strategy also portrayed organised labour as hostile to the national interest.[23] Despite the setbacks in the decade before 1914, the Conservatives were able to dominate the politics of the twentieth century in much the same way that the Liberals had been able to dominate the nineteenth.

Radicalism and conservatism were both based on a culture that celebrated the mythology of Englishness. How this mythology was appropriated determined the differing political loyalties of the nineteenth century. The nation is no doubt an 'imagined community' but its role in politics has frequently been decisive.

Conclusion

Towards post-revisionism

Ours is very much a subject in flux. At present anything that smacks of reductionism is out; ambiguity is in. The clarity of the narrative presented by the old analysis (elaborated in Chapter Two) has been contested and replaced by a story whose outlines are far from clear. Where historians once focused on politics and class society, they now offer a multi-stranded narrative. Class is no longer the sole determinant of political language and action. We have seen how religion, gender, national identity and the political process itself shaped popular experience. The intellectual spirit of our age is now beginning to question whether even these other forces of determination are themselves adequate. Can politics be related to wider historical forces at all? It starts to look as though we are simply left with a series of events, personalities and ideas that are typical of nothing but themselves. So where do we go from here? Does the old analysis, influenced as it was by socialism, have any relevance in a post-socialist world? What would a post-revisionist interpretation of popular politics look like?

The logic of this book suggests the following agenda. First of all, political history and the political realm should be reclaimed as integral to social history. We need to take high politics seriously so as to consider the ways in which the peculiarities of politics helped structure identity. The nature of the state, the franchise and party formation had social consequences. A certain amount of popular behaviour was contingent on events in the political realm (for example, the feeling of working-class exclusion after the Reform Act of 1832). But politics does not just mean high politics; it is also part of everyday life. Social issues such as poverty and wages were transformed by political language. This is not therefore an argument for returning to old-fashioned, Westminster-based political history. A narrow focus on politics involves a diminished view of the social and the personal. What is necessary is an expanded social history. Robert Gray persuasively argues that the enduring value of social history is that it shows what is not represented in the political sphere.[1] We need to explore the limitations of political ideology in different social contexts and the tensions within it. Politics is about the distribution of power; therefore social history cannot be complete without a political dimension whilst politics needs to be situated in social terms.

Second, the idea that popular politics can be explained without reference to class is a non-starter. But politics cannot be reduced to class either. A Marxist perspective would lead us to expect that popular politics in the nineteenth century was based on the conflict between the middle and working classes. Although this sometimes happened, much of the period under discussion saw the middle and working classes uniting as 'the people' against the allegedly corrupt aristocracy. Politics frequently cut across the classes. Nevertheless, class did determine the range of life opportunities and political choices available to an individual. Class was constructed both through the operation of the market and through political debate. The political realm (in the form of radicalism) interpreted the inequality of the market in class terms but the class system was also something that was felt and experienced both at a local and an individual level. What has not changed during this period of revisionism is the essential story about power and the loss of control over production by workers that characterised the nineteenth century. We now see that popular negotiations with the power bloc were sometimes contests over class inequality but they could also take other forms as well. Workers could be actively concerned about the treatment of their class and yet trumpet their attachment to the nation.

This suggests, third, that social and political identity is complex and fractured. Political activity was based on the deployment of a repertoire of forms of self identification: the identities of worker, elector (or non-elector), tax payer (even if the taxes were paid indirectly) or member of humanity. Religion shaped political culture and was often more relevant to individuals than the question of the vote. Class was one of many forms of identity. Modern social history is increasingly about the ways in which these forms of identity are appropriated and defined in different social settings.

Fourth, politics is a gendered process. This does not simply mean the involvement or absence of women in politics. Rather, gender and assumptions about gender underpinned all of social life. Citizenship was defined in male terms during the century although this was sometimes contested by women. When radical leaders spoke about the 'rights of man', they meant just that.

Fifth, language and techniques of representation are an integral part of the political process. Historians therefore have much to learn from the so-called 'linguistic turn' (the insights of post-structuralism and post-modernism). At the moment it seems that we are being offered a straight form of empirical social history on the one hand contrasted with the extreme relativism of post-modernity which undermines all historical claims to truth on the other. This is a false choice. Language (and political language) shaped experience and helped determine possible action. For example, we now see that the ways in which Victorians came to construct what they perceived as 'society' was not natural or inevitable but problematic and contested, subject to the explanatory power of language.[2] But this does not negate the social history that was intrinsic to the old analysis. The linguistic turn has yet to produce narratives of the past that are vastly different from what we already have and is weak on explaining change. Historians have been challenged by the linguistic turn on the question of whether society exists outside of language or whether we can only write about texts. We might respond that historians are in the business of retrieving a pre-existing reality (or, at least, recreating possible pasts subject to debate and the rules of evidence) but that reality is shaped by language. Social historians will continue to reconstruct the experience of people in the past and to highlight the social context of events. They will, however, build on past achievements by considering the forms of language and symbol available at any historical moment.[3] Like identity, language and cultural signs are unstable and open to subversion and contestation. For example, the language of constitutionalism pervaded radical discourse because of its elasticity; it evoked patriotism and the possibility of orderly change but also contained the hint of revolution. Historians have begun to concentrate on the ways in which political symbols and forms of expression were deployed and, importantly, the consequences of their use.[4] Language was not just a product of wider social forces; it helped create them by determining the range of possibilities available at any given time.

Finally, a post-revisionist agenda should endeavour to keep the people and ordinary experience in the historical record. The noblest part of the old analysis was its attempt to allow people in the past to speak for themselves, hence the preoccupation with working-class autobiography. We now see (thanks to the linguistic turn) that this evidence is complex. People do not simply tell their own stories. These stories are shaped by linguistic codes and conventions (for example, narratives about self-improvement). The stories that people encountered in melodramatic fiction or the popular belief in a lost golden age helped shape their world views. However, people are more than the texts they read and write. The techniques of revisionism have located rhetorical strategies that were integral to mass communication and helped isolate political ideas, but we need to allow for idiosyncrasy and emotions and be prepared for people in the past to act in surprising and unconventional ways. Revisionism is itself subject to the perils of reductionism. The creativity of people in the past and their ability to shape their own destiny within historical limits (the problem of 'agency') should remain at the core of any serious approach to our subject.

The literature on the Queen Caroline affair illustrates the opportunities for new ways of thinking about popular politics, incorporating gender and national identity. Class and the inequalities created by the capitalist mode of production have not disappeared from the account but if we are to understand the nature of class society, we must investigate how social relations were mediated by other factors. The purpose of post-revisionism will be to provide a social history of politics. Unashamedly, it will hold that there is such a thing as society.

Notes

1 REINTERPRETING THE QUEEN CAROLINE CASE

1 T.W. Laqueur, 'The Queen Caroline Affair: Politics as art in the reign of George IV', *Journal of Modern History*, 1982, vol. 54, pp. 434–5.
2 D. Thompson, 'Queen Victoria, the Monarchy and Gender' in her *Outsiders: Class, gender and nation*, London, Verso, 1993, p. 172.
3 Public Record Office: Home Office Papers 40/15 f. 15,129,148,177,186.
4 E.P. Thompson, *The Making of the English Working Class*, London, Penguin, 1968 (1963), p. 778. Thompson later revised his view of the Queen Caroline case: see Thompson's 'The Very Type of the "Respectable Artisan"', *New Society*, 3 May 1979, p. 276.
5 D. Wahrman, '"Middle-Class" Domesticity Goes Public: Gender, class and politics from Queen Caroline to Queen Victoria', *Journal of British Studies*, 1993, vol. 32, p. 404.
6 L. Davidoff and C. Hall, *Family Fortunes: Men and women of the English middle class, 1780–1850*, London, Hutchinson, 1987, pp. 149–55.
7 I. J. Prothero, *Artisans and Politics in Early Nineteenth-Century London: John Gast and his times*, Folkestone, Dawson, 1979, ch. 7.
8 *The Queen and Magna Charta; Or, the Thing that John signed*, London, 1820, pp. 24–5.
9 *The Queen and Magna Charta*, p. 11.
10 T.W. Laqueur, 'The Queen Caroline Affair', p. 442; T. Hunt, 'Morality and Monarchy in the Queen Caroline Affair', *Albion*, 1991, vol. 23, p. 716.
11 L. Colley, *Britons: Forging the nation 1707–1837*, New Haven, CT, and London, Yale University Press, 1992, p. 267.
12 A. Clark, 'Queen Caroline and the Sexual Politics of Popular Culture in London, 1820', *Representations*, 1990, no. 31, pp. 47–68; idem, *The Struggle for the Breeches: Gender and the making of the British working class*, London, Rivers Oram Press, 1995, ch. 9.
13 J. Gillis, *For Better, For Worse: British marriages, 1600 to the present*, New York, Oxford University Press, 1985, p. 223.
14 M. Girouard, *The Return to Camelot: Chivalry and the English gentleman*, New Haven, CT, and London, Yale University Press, 1981, p. 68.
15 T.W. Laqueur, 'The Queen Caroline Affair', p. 463.
16 C. Calhoun, *The Question of Class Struggle: Social foundations of*

popular radicalism during the Industrial Revolution, Chicago, IL, University of Chicago Press, 1982, pp. 105–15.

17 T.W. Laqueur, 'The Queen Caroline Affair'; A. Clark, 'Queen Caroline and the Sexual Politics of Popular Culture'.

18 I. McCalman, 'Unrespectable Radicalism: Infidels and pornography in early nineteenth-century London', *Past and Present*, 1984, no. 104, pp. 84–6; idem, *Radical Underworld: Prophets, revolutionaries and pornographers in London, 1795–1840*, Cambridge, Cambridge University Press, 1988, p. 205.

19 J. Fulcher, 'The Loyalist Response to the Queen Caroline Agitation', *Journal of British Studies*, 1995, vol. 34, pp. 481–502.

2 FROM THE OLD ANALYSIS TO THE NEW

1 For example, M. Ostrogorski, *Democracy and the Organisation of Political Parties*, London, 1902; S. Maccoby, *English Radicalism*, London, 1935–61, 6 vols; F. Gillespie, *Labor and Politics in England, 1850–1867*, Durham, NC, 1927; J. Robb, *The Primrose League, 1883–1906*, London, 1942.

2 M. Hovell, *The Chartist Movement*, Manchester, 1918.

3 G.D.H. Cole, *A Short History of the British Working-Class Movement, 1789–1947*, London, George Allen & Unwin, 1948.

4 E.J. Hobsbawm, *The Age of Revolution: Europe, 1789–1848*, London, Weidenfeld & Nicolson, 1962, p. xv.

5 G.D.H. Cole, *A Short History of the British Working-Class Movement*, p. 94.

6 J. Foster, *Class Struggle and the Industrial Revolution: Early industrial capitalism in three English towns*, London, Weidenfeld & Nicolson, 1974.

7 H. Kaye, *The British Marxist Historians: An introductory analysis*, Cambridge, Polity Press, 1984; B. Schwarz, '"The People" in History: The Communist Party Historians' Group, 1946–56' in R. Johnson *et al.* (eds), *Making Histories: Studies in history-writing and politics*, London, Hutchinson, 1982, pp. 44–95. For other influences on post-war social history, see M. Taylor, 'The Beginnings of Modern British Social History?', *History Workshop Journal*, 1997, no. 43, pp. 155–76.

8 E.P. Thompson, 'The Moral Economy of the English Crowd in the Eighteenth Century', *Past and Present*, 1971, no. 50, pp. 76–136; E.J. Hobsbawm and G. Rudé, *Captain Swing*, London, Lawrence & Wishart, 1969.

9 E.P. Thompson, *The Making of the English Working Class*, London, Penguin, 1968 (1963), pp. 9–10.

10 D. Fraser, *Urban Politics in Victorian England*, Leicester, Leicester University Press, 1976; E.P. Hennock, *Fit and Proper Persons: Ideal and reality in nineteenth-century urban government*, London, Arnold, 1973.

11 E.J. Hobsbawm, 'The Making of the Working Class, 1870–1914' in his *Worlds of Labour: Further studies in the history of labour*, London, Weidenfeld & Nicolson, 1984, pp. 194–213.

12 J.F.C. Harrison, *Early Victorian Britain*, London, Fontana, 1979 (1971), pp. 42, 186.

13 J. Lawrence and M. Taylor, 'Introduction: Electoral sociology and the historians' in J. Lawrence and M. Taylor (eds) *Party, State and Society: Electoral behaviour in Britain since 1820*, London, Scolar Press, 1997, pp. 1–26.

14 C.R. Dod, *Electoral Facts from 1832 to 1852, Impartially Stated*, London, 1852.

15 D.C. Moore, *The Politics of Deference: A study of the mid-nineteenth century English political system*, Hassocks, Harvester Press, 1976.

16 H.J. Hanham, *Elections and Party Management*, Hassocks, Harvester Press, 1978 (1959), p. xii; J.R. Vincent, *The Formation of the Liberal Party, 1857–1868*, London, Constable, 1966.

17 H. Pelling, *Social Geography of British Elections, 1885–1910*, London, Macmillan, 1967.

18 P.F. Clarke, *Lancashire and the New Liberalism*, Cambridge, Cambridge University Press, 1971; *idem*, 'Electoral Sociology of Modern Britain', *History*, 1972, vol. 7, pp. 31–55.

19 A.P. Donajgrodski (ed.), *Social Control in Nineteenth-Century Britain*, London, Croom Helm, 1977.

20 E.P. Thompson, *Whigs and Hunters: The origin of the Black Act*, London, Penguin, 1977 (1975), pp. 263–4.

21 E.J. Hobsbawm, 'The Labour Aristocracy in Nineteenth-Century Britain' in his *Labouring Men*, London, Weidenfeld & Nicolson, 1964, pp. 272–315.

22 R. Gray, *The Labour Aristocracy in Victorian Edinburgh*, Oxford, Clarendon Press, 1976; G. Crossick, *An Artisan Elite in Victorian Society: Kentish London, 1840–1880*, London, Croom Helm, 1978.

23 H. Pelling, 'Labour and the Downfall of Liberalism' in his *Popular Politics and Society in Late Victorian Britain*, London, Macmillan, 1968, pp. 101–20; K. Laybourn, 'The Rise of Labour and the Decline of Liberalism: The state of the debate', *History*, 1995, vol. 80, pp.207–26.

24 J. Saville, *The Labour Movement in Britain: A commentary*, London, Faber, 1988.

25 G. Best, 'The Making of the English Working Class', *Historical Journal*, 1965, vol. 8, p. 278.

26 K. Boyd and R. McWilliam, 'Historical Perspectives on Class and Culture', *Social History*, 1995, vol. 20, pp. 93–100.

27 See A. Hughes, *The Causes of the English Civil War*, London, Macmillan, 1991; G. Lewis, *The French Revolution: Rethinking the debate*, London, Routledge, 1993.

28 N.F.R. Crafts, *British Economic Growth during the Industrial Revolution*, Oxford, Clarendon Press, 1985; Pat Hudson's *The Industrial Revolution*, London, Arnold, 1992, is a masterly post-revisionist survey of the current literature.

29 G.S. Jones, 'Re-thinking Chartism' in his *Languages of Class: Studies in English working-class history, 1832–1982*, Cambridge, Cambridge University Press, 1983, pp. 90–178.

30 N. Rogers, *Whigs and Cities: Popular politics in the age of Walpole and Pitt*, Oxford, Clarendon Press, 1989; K. Wilson, *The Sense of the People: Politics, culture and imperialism in England, 1715–1785*, Cambridge, Cambridge University Press, 1995.

31 S. Rowbotham, *Hidden from History: 300 years of women's oppression and the fight against it*, London, Pluto Press, 1974; D. Thompson, 'Women and Nineteenth-Century Radical Politics: A lost dimension' in her *Outsiders: Class, gender and nation*, London, Verso, 1993, pp. 77–102.

32 J. Schwarzkopf, *Women in the Chartist Movement*, London, Macmillan, 1991; A. Clark, *The Struggle for the Breeches: Gender and the making of the British working class*, London, Rivers Oram, 1995.

33 M. Pugh, *The Tories and the People 1880–1935*, Oxford, Blackwell, 1985; L. Colley, *Britons: Forging the nation, 1707–1837*, New Haven, CT, and London, Yale University Press, 1991.

34 P. Joyce, 'The End of Social History?', *Social History*, 1995, vol. 20, pp. 73–91; see also L. Hunt (ed.), *The New Cultural History*, Berkeley, CA, University of California Press, 1989.

35 J.W. Scott, 'The Evidence of Experience', *Critical Inquiry*, 1991, vol. 17, pp. 773–97.

36 I. Dyck, *William Cobbett and Rural Popular Culture*, Cambridge, Cambridge University Press, 1992; A. Howkins, *Poor Labouring Men*, London, Routledge, 1985; M. Reed and R. Wells (eds), *Class, Conflict and Protest in the English Countryside, 1700–1880*, London, Cass, 1990.

37 J. Belchem, *Popular Radicalism in Nineteenth Century Britain*, London, Macmillan, 1996; J. Epstein, *Radical Expression: Political language, ritual, and symbol in England, 1790–1850*, New York, Oxford University Press, 1994.

3 THE PECULIARITIES OF POLITICS

1 A. Wilson (ed.), *Rethinking Social History: English society 1570–1920 and its interpretation*, Manchester, Manchester University Press, 1993.

2 I.J. Prothero, *Artisans and Politics in Early Nineteenth-century London: John Gast and his times*, Folkestone, Dawson, 1979, ch. 14.

3 J.R. Vincent, *Pollbooks*, Cambridge, Cambridge University Press, 1967, p. 33.

4 P.J. Corfield (ed.), *Language, History and Class*, Oxford, Blackwell, 1991.

5 K. Marx and F. Engels, *The Manifesto of the Communist Party*, Moscow, Progress Publishers, 1952 (1848), p. 44.

6 B. Jessop, *The Capitalist State: Marxist theories and methods*, Oxford, Robertson, 1982.

7 P.B. Evans, D. Rueschmeyer and T. Skocpol (eds), *Bringing the State Back In*, Cambridge, Cambridge University Press, 1985, p. viii.

8 G.S. Jones, 'Rethinking Chartism', in his *Languages of Class: Studies in English working-class history, 1832–1982*, Cambridge, Cambridge University Press, 1983, pp. 90–178.

9 F. Furet, *Interpreting the French Revolution*, Cambridge, Cambridge University Press, 1981 (1978); W.H. Sewell, Jnr, *Work and Revolution in France: The language of labor from the Old Regime to 1848*, Cambridge, Cambridge University Press, 1980. See also L. Berlanstein (ed.), *Rethinking Labor History: Essays on discourse and class analysis*, Urbana, IL, University of Illinois Press, 1993.

10 For example, E.F. Biagini, *Liberty, Retrenchment and Reform: Popular*

Liberalism in the age of Gladstone, 1860–1880, Cambridge, Cambridge University Press, 1992; E.F. Biagini and A.J. Reid (eds), *Currents of Radicalism: Popular radicalism, organised labour and party politics in Britain, 1850–1914*, Cambridge, Cambridge University Press, 1991; D. Feldman, *Englishmen and Jews: Social relations and political culture, 1840–1914*, New Haven, CT, and London, Yale University Press, 1994; J. Lawrence, 'Popular Radicalism and the Socialist Revival in Britain', *Journal of British Studies*, 1994, vol. 31, pp. 163–86; A.J. Reid, *Social Classes and Social Relations in Britain, 1850–1914*, London, Macmillan, 1992; D. Tanner, *Political Change and the Labour Party, 1900–1918*, Cambridge, Cambridge University Press, 1990; M. Taylor, *The Decline of British Radicalism, 1847–1860*, Oxford, Clarendon Press, 1995; D. Wahrman, *Imagining the Middle Class: The political representation of class in Britain, c.1780–1840*, Cambridge, Cambridge University Press, 1995.

11 P. Joyce, *Visions of the People: Industrial England and the question of class, 1840–1914*, Cambridge, Cambridge University Press, 1990.

12 Amongst the many replies, see J. Epstein, 'Rethinking the Categories of Working-Class History', *Labour/Le Travail*, 1986, vol. 18, pp. 195–208; R. Gray, 'The Deconstructing of the English Working Class', *Social History*, 1986, vol. 11, pp. 363–73; N. Kirk, 'In Defence of Class: A critique of recent revisionist writing upon the nineteenth century working class', *International Review of Social History*, 1987, vol. 32, pp. 2–47; J.W. Scott, 'On Language, Gender and Working-Class History', *International Labor and Working-Class History*, 1987, no. 31, pp. 1–13. See also D. Mayfield and S. Thorne, 'Social History and its Discontents: Gareth Stedman Jones and the politics of language', *Social History*, 1992, vol. 17, pp. 165–88; J. Lawrence and M. Taylor, 'The Poverty of Protest: Gareth Stedman Jones and the politics of language – a reply', *Social History*, 1993, vol. 18, pp. 1–15.

4 A POLITY-CENTRED HISTORY? RETHINKING THE STATE, THE FRANCHISE AND PARTY FORMATION

1 T. Skocpol, 'Bringing the State Back In: Strategies of analysis in current research' in P.B. Evans, D. Rueschmeyer and T. Skocpol (eds), *Bringing the State back in*, Cambridge, Cambridge University Press, 1985, p. 25.

2 L. Davison *et al.* (eds), *Stilling the Grumbling Hive: The response to social and economic problems in England, 1689–1750*, Stroud, Alan Sutton, 1992.

3 P. Thane, 'Government and Society in England and Wales, 1750–1914' in F.M.L. Thompson (ed.), *The Cambridge Social History of Britain, 1750–1950*, Cambridge, Cambridge University Press, 1990, vol. 3, pp. 1–61 is a useful survey of state formation.

4 J. Prest, *Liberty and Locality: Parliament, permissive legislation and ratepayers' democracies in the nineteenth century*, Oxford, Clarendon Press, 1990.

5 D. Eastwood, *Governing Rural England: Tradition and transformation in local government, 1789–1840*, Oxford, Clarendon Press, 1994, p. 2.

6 J. Brewer, *The Sinews of Power: War, money and the English state, 1688–1783*, London, Unwin Hyman, 1989.

7 E.P. Thompson, *The Making of the English Working Class*, London, Penguin, 1968 (1963), p. 661.

8 P. Harling and P. Mandler, 'From "Fiscal-Military" State to Laissez-Faire State, 1760–1850', *Journal of British Studies*, 1993, vol. 32, pp. 44–70.

9 P. Harling, 'Rethinking "Old Corruption"', *Past and Present*, 1995, no. 147, pp. 127–58.

10 H.C.G. Matthew, *Gladstone, 1809–1874*, Oxford, Oxford University Press, 1988, ch. 5.

11 V.A.C. Gatrell, 'Crime, Authority and the Policeman-State' in F.M.L. Thompson (ed.), *The Cambridge Social History of Britain*, vol. 3, pp. 243–310.

12 J. Saville, *1848: The British state and the Chartist movement*, Cambridge, Cambridge University Press, 1987.

13 R. McWilliam, 'The Mysteries of G.W.M. Reynolds: Radicalism and melodrama in Victorian Britain' in M. Chase and I. Dyck (eds), *Living and Learning: Essays in honour of J.F.C. Harrison*, London, Scolar Press, 1996, pp. 182–98.

14 M. Langan and B. Schwarz (eds), *Crises in the British State, 1880–1930*, London, Hutchinson, 1985.

15 J. Walkowitz, *Prostitution and Victorian Society: Women, class and the state*, Cambridge, Cambridge University Press, 1980.

16 H. Pelling, 'The Working Class and the Origins of the Welfare State' in his *Popular Politics and Society in Late Victorian Britain*, London, Macmillan, 1968, pp. 1–18; P. Thane, 'The Working Class and State "Welfare" in Britain, 1880–1914', *Historical Journal*, 1984, vol. 27, pp. 877–900.

17 J. Habermas, *The Structural Transformation of the Public Sphere: An inquiry into a category of bourgeois society*, Cambridge, Polity Press, 1989 (1962). See also C. Calhoun (ed.), *Habermas and the Public Sphere*, Cambridge, MA, MIT Press, 1993.

18 D. Wahrman, *Imagining the Middle Class: The political representation of class in Britain, c. 1780–1840*, Cambridge, Cambridge University Press, 1995, ch. 9–10.

19 A.V. Dicey, 'The Balance of Classes' in *Essays on Reform*, London, 1867, pp. 82–3.

20 F. O'Gorman, *Voters, Patrons and Parties: The unreformed electoral system of Hanoverian England, 1734–1832*, Oxford, Oxford University Press, 1989; J.A. Phillips, *Electoral Behaviour in Unreformed England: Plumpers, splitters and straights*, Princeton, NJ, Princeton University Press, 1982; J. Vernon, *Politics and the People: A study in English political culture, c.1815–1867*, Cambridge, Cambridge University Press, 1983.

21 See D. Beales, 'The Electorate Before and After 1832: The right to vote and the opportunity', *Parliamentary History*, 1992, vol. 11, pp. 139–50 and the reply by F. O'Gorman, 'The Electorate Before and After 1832', *Parliamentary History*, 1993, vol. 12, pp. 171–83.

22 J. Davis, 'Slums and the Vote, 1867–90', *Historical Research*, 1991, vol. 64, pp. 375–88; D. Tanner, *Political Change and the Labour Party, 1900–1918*, Cambridge, Cambridge University Press, 1990; H.C.G.

Matthew, R. McKibbin and J.A. Kay, 'The Franchise Factor in the Rise of the Labour Party', *English Historical Review*, 1976, vol. 91, pp. 723–52.

23 E. Yeo, 'Some practices and problems of Chartist Democracy' in J. Epstein and D. Thompson (eds), *The Chartist Experience: Studies in working-class radicalism and culture, 1830–60*, London, Macmillan, 1982, pp. 345–80.

24 G. Eley, 'Edward Thompson, Social History and Political Culture: The making of a working-class public, 1780–1850' in H.J. Kaye and K. McClelland (eds), *E.P. Thompson: Critical perspectives*, London, Polity Press, 1990, pp. 12–49.

25 F. O'Gorman, 'Campaign Rituals and Ceremonies: The social meaning of elections in England, 1780–1860', *Past and Present*, 1992, no. 135, pp. 72–115; J. Vernon, *Politics and the People*.

26 J. Vernon, *Politics and the People*, pp. 171–2.

27 V. Hart, *Democracy and Distrust: Political distrust in Britain and America*, Cambridge, Cambridge University Press, 1978, ch. 4; J. Lawrence, 'Popular Politics and the Limitations of Party: Wolverhampton, 1867–1900' in E.F. Biagini and A.J. Reid (eds), *Currents of Radicalism: Popular radicalism, organised labour and party politics in Britain, 1850–1914*, Cambridge, Cambridge University Press, 1991, pp. 65–85.

28 J. Vernon, *Politics and the People*, pp. 186–7.

29 J.G.A. Pocock, *Virtue, Commerce and History: Essays on political thought and history, chiefly in the eighteenth century*, Cambridge, Cambridge University Press, 1985.

30 P. Mandler, *Aristocratic Government in the Age of Reform: Whigs and Liberals, 1830–52*, Oxford, Clarendon Press, 1990, ch. 1.

31 H.C.G. Matthew, 'Rhetoric and Politics in Great Britain, 1860–1950' in P.J. Waller (ed.), *Politics and Social Change in Modern Britain: Essays presented to A.F. Thompson*, Brighton, Harvester Press, 1987, pp. 34–58.

32 J. Lawrence and M. Taylor, (eds), *Party, State and Society: Electoral behaviour in Britain since 1820*, London, Scolar Press, 1997.

33 P. Pickering, *Chartism and the Chartists in Manchester and Salford*, London, Macmillan, 1995, ch. 8.

34 P. Pickering, *Chartism and the Chartists in Manchester*, ch. 9.

35 M. Taylor, 'Rethinking the Chartists: Searching for synthesis in the historiography of Chartism', *Historical Journal*, 1996, vol. 39, pp. 479–95.

36 O. Smith, *The Politics of Language, 1791–1819*, Oxford, Clarendon Press, 1984.

5 THE CULTURE OF POPULAR RADICALISM I: POPULISM, CLASS AND THE CONSTITUTION

1 I.J. Prothero, *Artisans and Politics in Early Nineteenth-century London: John Gast and his times*, Folkestone, Dawson, 1979.

2 G. Ionescu and E. Gellner (eds), *Populism: Its meanings and national characteristics*, London, Weidenfeld & Nicolson, 1969.

3 M. Canovan, *Populism*, London, Junction Books, 1981.

4 C. Calhoun, *The Question of Class Struggle: Social foundations of*

popular radicalism during the Industrial Revolution, Chicago, IL, University of Chicago Press, 1982; P. Joyce, *Visions of the People: Industrial England and the question of class, 1870–1914*, Cambridge, Cambridge University Press, 1990; see also M. Roe, *Kenealy and the Tichborne Cause: A study in mid-Victorian populism*, Melbourne, Melbourne University Press, 1974, ch. 7.

5 P. Joyce, *Visions of the People*, p. 15, original emphases.

6 P. Joyce, *Democratic Subjects: The self and the social in nineteenth century England*, Cambridge, Cambridge University Press, 1994.

7 W.D. Rubinstein, 'British Radicalism and the "Dark Side" of Populism' in his *Elites and the Wealthy in Modern British History: Essays in social and economic history*, Brighton, Harvester Press, 1987, pp. 339–73.

8 W. Hazlitt, 'What is the People?' in P.P. Howe (ed.), *The Complete Works of William Hazlitt*, London, Dent, 1932, vol. 7, p. 26.

9 *The Pioneer*, 28 June 1834, p. 413, original emphasis.

10 I.J. Prothero, 'William Benbow and the Concept of the General Strike', *Past and Present*, 1974, no. 63, p. 142; J. Epstein, *The Lion of Freedom: Feargus O'Connor and the Chartist movement, 1832–1842*, London, Croom Helm, 1982, p. 90.

11 D. Thompson, 'Who were "the People" in 1842?' in M. Chase and I. Dyck (eds), *Living and Learning: Essays in honour of J.F.C. Harrison*, London, Scolar Press, 1996, pp. 118–32.

12 A. Briggs, 'The Language of "Mass" and "Masses" in Nineteenth-Century England' in D.E. Martin and D. Rubinstein (eds), *Ideology and the Labour Movement: Essays presented to John Saville*, London, Croom Helm, 1974, pp. 62–83.

13 *Bill of Pains and Penalties, 1820* in Home Office Papers 40/14 f.49 (Public Record Office).

14 C. Hindley, *Curiosities of Street Literature*, London, 1871, vol. I, p. 116.

15 J. Belchem, 'Republicanism, Popular Constitutionalism and the Radical Platform in Early Nineteenth-Century England', *Social History*, 1981, vol. 6, pp. 1–32; J. Vernon (ed.), *Re-reading the Constitution: New narratives in the political history of England's long nineteenth century*, Cambridge, Cambridge University Press, 1996.

16 E.F. Biagini, *Liberty, Retrenchment and Reform: Popular Liberalism in the age of Gladstone, 1860–1880*, Cambridge, Cambridge University Press, 1992, p. 43.

17 C. Hill, 'The Norman Yoke' in J. Saville (ed.), *Democracy and the Labour Movement: Essays in honour of Dona Torr*, London, Lawrence & Wishart, 1954, pp. 11–66.

18 *Reynolds's Political Instructor*, 10 November 1849, p. 5, original emphasis.

19 *De Morgan's Monthly*, 1 May 1877, p. 39.

20 A. Howkins and I. Dyck, '"The Time's Alteration": Popular ballads, rural radicalism and William Cobbett', *History Workshop Journal*, 1987, no. 23, pp. 20–38.

21 R. Samuel, 'The Discovery of Puritanism, 1820–1914: A preliminary sketch' in J. Garnett and C. Matthew (eds), *Revival and Religion since 1700: Essays for John Walsh*, London, Hambledon Press, 1993, pp. 201–47.

22 J. Epstein, 'Understanding the Cap of Liberty: Symbolic practice and social conflict in early nineteenth-century England' in his *Radical Expression: Political language, ritual and symbol in England, 1790–1850*, New York, Oxford University Press, 1994, pp. 70–99.

23 M.W. Steinberg, '"The Labour of the Country is the Wealth of the Country": Class identity, consciousness and the role of discourse in the making of the English working class', *International Labor and Working-Class History*, 1996, no. 49, p. 16.

24 F. O'Connor (ed.), *The Trial of Feargus O'Connor . . . and Fifty-eight Others . . . on a Charge of Sedition, Conspiracy, Tumult, and Riot*, London, 1843, pp. 254–5.

25 N. Thompson, *The People's Science: The popular political economy of exploitation and crisis, 1816–34*, Cambridge, Cambridge University Press, 1984.

26 D. Thompson, *The Chartists: Popular politics in the Industrial Revolution*, London, Temple Smith, 1984; *idem*, 'Chartism and the Historians' in her *Outsiders: Class, gender and nation*, London, Verso, 1993, pp. 19–44.

27 P. Hollis, *The Pauper Press*, Oxford, Oxford University Press, 1970.

28 M. Chase, *The People's Farm: English radical agrarianism, 1775–1840*, Oxford, Clarendon Press, 1988; *idem*, '"We Wish Only To Work For Ourselves": The Chartist Land Plan' in M. Chase and I. Dyck (eds), *Living and Learning*, pp. 133–48; H. Perkin, 'Land Reform and Class Conflict in Victorian Britain' in his *The Structured Crowd: Essays in British social history*, Brighton, Harvester, 1981, pp. 100–35.

29 M.C. Finn, *After Chartism: Class and nation in English radical politics, 1848–74*, Cambridge, Cambridge University Press, 1993, ch. 2.

30 I. McCalman, *Radical Underworld: Prophets, revolutionaries and pornographers in London, 1795–1840*, Cambridge, Cambridge University Press, 1988.

31 E. Royle, *Victorian Infidels: The origins of the British secularist movement, 1791–1880*, Manchester, Manchester University Press, 1974; D. Nash, *Secularism, Art and Freedom*, Leicester, Leicester University Press, 1992.

32 C. Waters, *British Socialists and the Politics of Popular Culture, 1884–1914*, Manchester, Manchester University Press, 1990.

33 J.F.C. Harrison, *The Second Coming: Popular millenarianism, 1780–1850*, London, Routledge & Kegan Paul, 1979.

34 E. Yeo, 'Christianity in Chartist Struggle, 1838–1842', *Past and Present*, 1981, no. 91, p. 109.

35 E. Evans, 'The Church in Danger?: Anti-Clericalism in nineteenth-century England', *European Studies Review*, 1983, vol. 13, pp. 201–24; E.F. Biagini, *Liberty, Retrenchment and Reform*, ch. 4.

36 B. Harrison, *Drink and the Victorians: The temperance question in England, 1815–1872*, London, Faber & Faber, 1971.

37 J. Epstein, 'Rituals of Solidarity: Radical dining, toasting and symbolic expression' in his *Radical Expression*, pp. 147–65.

38 P. Pickering, *Chartism and the Chartists in Manchester and Salford*, London, Macmillan, 1995, ch. 8.

39 J. Belchem, *'Orator' Hunt: Henry Hunt and English working-class radicalism*, Oxford, Clarendon Press, 1985; J. Epstein, *The Lion of Freedom*;

J. Belchem and J. Epstein, 'The Nineteenth-Century Gentleman Leader Revisited', *Social History*, 1997, vol. 22, pp. 174–93.

40 I.J. Prothero, 'William Benbow and the concept of the "General Strike"'.

41 P. Taylor, *Popular Politics in Early Industrial Britain: Bolton, 1825–1850*, Keele, Ryburn Publishing, 1995; M. Winstanley, 'Oldham Radicalism and the Origins of Popular Liberalism', *Historical Journal*, 1993, vol. 36, pp. 619–43.

42 E.F. Biagini and A.J. Reid (eds), *Currents of Radicalism: Popular radicalism, organised labour and party politics in Britain, 1850–1914*, Cambridge, Cambridge University Press, 1991.

43 J.R. Vincent, *The Formation of the Liberal Party, 1857–1868*, London, Constable, 1966.

44 E.F. Biagini, *Liberty, Retrenchment and Reform*.

45 J.P. Parry, *The Rise and Fall of Liberal Government in Victorian Britain*, New Haven, CT, Yale University Press, 1993.

46 M.C. Finn, *After Chartism*, chs 5–6.

47 R. McWilliam, 'Radicalism and Popular Culture: The Tichborne case and the politics of "fair play"' in E.F. Biagini and A.J. Reid (eds), *Currents of Radicalism*, pp. 44–64.

48 J. Belchem and J. Epstein, 'The Nineteenth-Century Gentleman Leader Revisited', *Social History*, 1997, vol. 22, pp. 174–93.

6 THE CULTURE OF POPULAR RADICALISM II: GENDER AND SOCIALISM

1 J.W. Scott, *Gender and the Politics of History*, New York, Columbia University Press, 1988.

2 S. Rose, *Limited Livelihoods: Gender and class in nineteenth-century England*, London, Routledge, 1992.

3 A. Vickery, 'Golden Age to Separate Spheres?: A review of the categories and chronology of English women's history', *Historical Journal*, 1993, vol. 36, pp. 383–414.

4 C. Midgely, *Women against Slavery: The British campaigns, 1780–1870*, London, Routledge, 1992.

5 Cited in B. Taylor, *Eve and the New Jerusalem*, London, Virago, 1983, p. 80.

6 S. Alexander, 'Women, Class and Sexual Differences in the 1830s and 1840s: Some reflections on the writing of a feminist history', *History Workshop Journal*, 1984, no. 17, pp. 125–49.

7 B. Taylor, *Eve and the New Jerusalem*.

8 A. Clark, *The Struggle for the Breeches: Gender and the making of the British working class*, London, Rivers Oram, 1995.

9 Cited in B. Taylor, *Eve and the New Jerusalem*, p. 75.

10 D. Thompson, 'Women and Nineteenth-Century Radical Politics: A lost dimension' in her *Outsiders: Class, gender and nation*, London, Verso, 1993, pp. 77–102.

11 J. Schwarzkopf, *Women in the Chartist Movement*, London, Macmillan, 1991, ch. 8.

12 P. Hollis, *Ladies Elect: Women in English local government, 1865–1914*, Oxford, Clarendon Press, 1987.

13 Cited in L. Walker, 'Party Political Women: A comparative study of Liberal women and the Primrose League, 1890–1914' in J. Rendall (ed.), *Equal or Different: Women's politics, 1800–1914*, Oxford, Basil Blackwell, 1987, p. 174.

14 J. Walkowitz, *City of Dreadful Delight: Narratives of sexual danger in late Victorian London*, London, Virago, 1992.

15 A. Clark, *The Struggle for the Breeches*, p. 3.

16 J. Schwarzkopf, *Women in the Chartist Movement*, p. 39.

17 J. Schwarzkopf, *Women in the Chartist Movement*, p. 45.

18 W. Seccombe, 'Patriarchy Stabilized: The construction of the male bread-winner wage norm in nineteenth-century Britain', *Social History*, 1986, vol. 11, pp. 53–76.

19 A. Clark, *The Struggle for the Breeches*, p. 271.

20 K. McClelland, 'Rational and Respectable Men: Gender, the working class, and citizenship in Britain, 1850–1867' in L.L. Frader and S.O. Rose (eds), *Gender and Class in Modern Europe*, Ithaca, NY, Cornell University Press, 1996, pp. 280–93; *idem*, 'Masculinity and the "Representative Artisan" in Britain, 1850–1880' in J. Tosh and M. Roper (eds), *Manful Assertions: Masculinities in Britain since 1800*, London, Routledge, 1991, pp. 74–91.

21 B.L. Kinzer, *The Ballot Question in Nineteenth Century English Politics*, New York, Garland, 1982.

22 K. Hunt, *Equivocal Feminists: The Social Democratic Federation and the woman question, 1884–1911*, Cambridge, Cambridge University Press, 1996.

23 T. Koditschek, 'The Gendering of the British Working Class', *Gender and History*, 1997, vol. 9, pp. 333–63, is a useful overview of recent research.

24 G.S. Jones, 'Working-class culture and working-class politics in London, 1870–1900: Notes on the remaking of a working class' in his *Languages of Class*, pp. 179–238; R. McKibbin, 'Why was there no Marxism in Britain?' in his *The Ideologies of Class: Social relations in Britain, 1880–1950*, Oxford, Oxford University Press, 1991, pp. 1–41.

25 C. Waters, *British Socialists and the Politics of Popular Culture, 1884–1914*, Manchester, Manchester University Press, 1990.

26 R. Roberts, *The Classic Slum: Salford life in the first quarter of the century*, Manchester, Manchester University Press, 1971, p. 14.

27 G. Claeys, *Citizens and Saints: Politics and anti-politics in early British socialism*, Cambridge, Cambridge University Press, 1989, ch. 1.

28 G. Claeys, *Machinery, Money and the Millennium: From moral economy to socialism, 1815–60*, Cambridge, Polity Press, 1987.

29 G. Claeys, *Citizens and Saints*, p. 320.

30 S. Shipley, *Club Life and Socialism in mid-Victorian London*, London, History Workshop, 1971.

31 J. Lawrence, 'Popular Radicalism and the Socialist Revival in Britain', *Journal of British Studies*, 1994, vol. 31, pp. 163–86.

32 M. Bevir, 'The British Social Democratic Federation, 1880–1885: From O'Brienism to Marxism', *International Review of Social History*, 1992, vol. 37, pp. 207–29.

33 L. Barrow and I. Bullock, *Democratic Ideas and the British Labour Movement, 1880–1918*, Cambridge, Cambridge University Press, 1996.
34 D. Howell, *British Workers and the Independent Labour Party, 1888–1906*, Manchester, Manchester University Press, 1983, pp. 352–62.
35 W.T. Stead, 'The Labour Party and the Books that Helped to Make It', *Review of Reviews*, 1906, vol. 33, pp. 568–82.
36 J. Davis, *Reforming London: The London government problem, 1855–1900*, Oxford, Oxford University Press, 1988; P. Thane, 'Labour and Local Politics: Radicalism, democracy and social reform, 1880–1914' in E.F. Biagini and A.J. Reid (eds), *Currents of Radicalism: Popular radicalism, organised labour and party politics in Britain, 1850–1914*, Cambridge, Cambridge University Press, 1991, pp. 244–70.
37 S. Yeo, 'A New Life: The religion of socialism in Britain, 1883–1896', *History Workshop Journal*, 1977, no. 4, pp. 5–56.
38 H.M. Hyndman and C. Bradlaugh, *Will Socialism Benefit the English People?*, London, 1884, p. 12.
39 P.J. Ward, *The Red Flag and the Union Jack*, forthcoming, 1998.

7 THE NATION AND POLITICS I: PATRIOTISM

1 T. Wright, *Our New Masters*, London, 1873, p. 16.
2 E.J. Hobsbawm, *Nations and Nationalism since 1780: Programme, myth, reality*, Cambridge, Cambridge University Press, 1992 (1990), ch. 1.
3 B. Anderson, *Imagined Communities: Reflections on the origins and spread of nationalism*, London, Verso, 1983.
4 E.J. Hobsbawm and T. Ranger (eds), *The Invention of Tradition*, Cambridge, Cambridge University Press, 1983.
5 G. Newman, *The Rise of English Nationalism: A cultural history, 1740–1830*, London, Weidenfeld & Nicolson, 1987, p. 52.
6 H. Kearney, *The British Isles: A history of four nations*, Cambridge, Cambridge University Press, 1989; J.G.A. Pocock, 'British History: A plea for a new subject', *Journal of Modern History*, 1975, vol. 47, pp. 601–28; R. Samuel, 'British Dimensions: Four nations history', *History Workshop Journal*, 1995, no. 40, pp. iii–xxii.
7 L. Colley, 'Britishness and Otherness: An argument', *Journal of British Studies*, 1992, vol. 31, pp. 309–29; see also E. Said, *Orientalism*, London, Routledge & Kegan Paul, 1978.
8 H. Pelling, 'British Labour and British Imperialism' in his *Popular Politics and Society in Late Victorian Britain*, London, Macmillan, 1968, pp. 82–100; R. Price, *An Imperial War and the British Working Class: Working-class attitudes and reactions to the Boer War, 1899–1902*, London, Routledge & Kegan Paul, 1972; *idem*, 'Society, Status and Jingoism: The social roots of lower middle-class patriotism, 1870–1900' in G. Crossick (ed.), *The Lower Middle Class in Britain, 1870–1914*, London, Croom Helm, 1977, pp. 89–112. See also H. Cunningham, 'Jingoism in 1877–78', *Victorian Studies*, 1971, vol. 14, pp. 429–53.
9 H. Cunningham, *The Volunteer Force: A social and political history 1859–1908*, London, Croom Helm, 1975, p. 122.
10 G.S. Jones, 'Working-Class Culture and Working-Class Politics in

London, 1870–1900' in his *Languages of Class: Studies in English working-class history, 1832–1902*, Cambridge, Cambridge University Press, 1983, pp. 179–238.

11 E.P. Thompson, *The Making of the English Working Class*, London, Penguin, 1968 (1963), ch. 4. For earlier attempts of left-wing historians to deal with the question of patriotism, see M. Taylor, 'Patriotism, History and the Left in Twentieth-Century Britain', *Historical Journal*, 1990, vol. 33, pp. 971–87.

12 For example, R. Samuel (ed.), *Patriotism: The making and unmaking of British national identity*, London, Routledge, 1989, 3 vols.; L. Colley, *Britons: Forging the nation, 1707–1837*, New Haven, CT and London, Yale University Press, 1992; R. Colls and P. Dodd (eds), *Englishness: Politics and Culture 1880–1920*, London, Croom Helm, 1986; E.J. Hobsbawm and T. Ranger (eds), *The Invention of Tradition*; T. Nairn, *The Enchanted Glass: Britain and its monarchy*, London, Hutchinson, 1986.

13 H. Cunningham, 'The Language of Patriotism, 1750–1914', *History Workshop Journal*, 1981, no. 12, pp. 8–33.

14 K. Wilson, *The Sense of the People: Politics, culture and imperialism in England, 1715–1785*, Cambridge, Cambridge University Press, 1995, ch. 3.

15 L. Colley, 'Radical Patriotism in Eighteenth Century England' in R. Samuel (ed.), *Patriotism* vol. 1, p. 182.

16 M. Taylor, 'John Bull and the Iconography of Public Opinion in England, c.1712–1929', *Past and Present*, 1992, no. 134, pp. 93–128.

17 R. Colls and P. Dodd (eds), *Englishness*.

18 J.A. Hobson, *The Psychology of Jingoism*, London, 1901.

19 M. Taylor, 'Patriotism, History and the Left', p. 987; *idem*, 'Imperium et Libertas?: Rethinking the Radical critique of imperialism during the nineteenth century', *Journal of Imperial and Commonwealth History*, 1991, vol. 19, pp. 1–23.

20 P.A. Pickering, *Chartism and the Chartists in Manchester and Salford*, London, Macmillan, 1995, p. 34.

21 G. Newman, *The Rise of English Nationalism*, p. 232.

22 M.C. Finn, *After Chartism: Class and nation in English radical politics, 1848–74*, Cambridge, Cambridge University Press, 1993, pp. 9–10.

23 A. Taylor, 'Palmerston and Radicalism, 1847–1865', *Journal of British Studies*, 1994, vol. 33, pp. 157–79.

24 J.H. Treble, 'O'Connor, O'Connell and the Attitudes of Irish Immigrants towards Chartism in the North of England, 1838–48' in J. Butt and I.F. Clarke (eds), *The Victorians and Social Protest: A symposium*, Newton Abbot, David & Charles, 1973, pp. 33–70; D. Thompson, 'Ireland and the Irish in England before 1850' in her *Outsiders: Class, gender and nation*, London, Verso, 1993, pp. 103–33.

25 J. Belchem, 'English Working-Class Radicalism and the Irish, 1815–50' in R. Swift and S. Gilley (eds), *The Irish in the Victorian City*, London, Croom Helm, 1985, pp. 85–97.

26 J. Belchem, 'English Working-Class Radicalism and the Irish', p. 91.

27 R. Gott, 'Little Englanders' in R. Samuel (ed.), *Patriotism*, vol. 1, pp. 90–102.

28 A.J.P. Taylor, *The Trouble Makers: Dissent over foreign policy*, London, Hamish Hamilton, 1957.
29 L. Colley, *Britons*, p. 30.
30 J. Wolffe, *God and Greater Britain: Religion and national life in Britain and Ireland, 1843–1945*, London, Routledge, 1994.
31 C. Hall. 'Competing Masculinities: Thomas Carlyle, John Stuart Mill and the Case of Governor Eyre' in her *White, Male and Middle Class: Explorations in feminism and history*, Cambridge, Polity Press, 1992, pp. 255–95.
32 C. Hall, 'Rethinking Imperial Histories: The Reform Act of 1867', *New Left Review*, 1994, no. 208, pp. 3–29.
33 G. Newman, *The Rise of English Nationalism*, pp. 129–32.
34 P. Furtado, 'National Pride in Seventeenth-Century England' in R. Samuel, *Patriotism*, vol. 1, p. 49.

8 THE NATION AND POLITICS II: POPULAR CONSERVATISM

1 B. Disraeli, *Speech of the Right Hon. B. Disraeli MP at the Banquet of the National Union of Conservative and Constitutional Associations*, London, 1872, pp. 6–7.
2 Cited in A.J.P. Taylor, *The Trouble Makers: Dissent over foreign policy*, London, Hamish Hamilton, 1957, p. 15.
3 R. Blake, *The Conservative Party From Peel to Thatcher*, London, Methuen, 1985 (1972), p. 21–2.
4 R.L. Hill, *Toryism and the People, 1832–1846*, London, 1929, ch. 2.
5 R.L. Hill, *Toryism and the People*, pp. 53–4.
6 M. Pugh, *The Tories and the People, 1880–1935*, Oxford, Blackwell, 1985, ch. 1.
7 P. Joyce, *Work, Society and Politics: The culture of the factory in later Victorian Britain*, Hassocks, Harvester, 1980, p. 185.
8 R. Roberts, *The Classic Slum: Salford life in the first quarter of the century*, Manchester, Manchester University Press, 1971, pp. 133–4.
9 E.H.H. Green, *The Crisis of Conservatism: The politics, economics, and ideology of the British Conservative Party, 1880–1914*, London, Routledge, 1995.
10 K. Marx and F. Engels, *The Manifesto of the Communist Party*, Moscow, Progress Publishers, 1952, pp. 57–8.
11 P. Joyce, *Work, Society and Politics*, p. 211.
12 P. Joyce, *Work, Society and Politics*.
13 P. Joyce, 'Popular Toryism in Lancashire, 1860–1890', unpublished D.Phil. thesis, University of Oxford, 1975, p. 371.
14 R. Roberts, *The Classic Slum*, p. 94.
15 A.J. Lee, 'Conservatism, Traditionalism and the British Working Class, 1880–1918' in D.E. Martin and D. Rubinstein (eds), *Ideology and the Labour Movement: Essays presented to John Saville*, London, Croom Helm, 1974, pp. 94–6.
16 M. Pugh, *The Tories and the People*, ch. 3; J. Lawrence, 'Class and Gender in the Making of Urban Toryism, 1880–1914', *English Historical*

Review, 1993, vol. 108, pp. 628–52; L. Walker, 'Party Political Women: A comparative study of Liberal women and the Primrose League, 1890–1914' in J. Rendall (ed.) *Equal or Different: Women's politics, 1800–1914*, Oxford, Blackwell, 1987, pp. 165–91.

17 V.S. Berridge, 'Popular Journalism and Working-Class Attitudes, 1854–1886', D.Phil. thesis, University of London, 1976, pp. 297–305.

18 J. Mackenzie, *Propaganda and Empire: The manipulation of British public opinion, 1880–1960*, Manchester, Manchester University Press, 1984.

19 *Speech of the Right Hon. B. Disraeli . . .* , p. 6.

20 D. Cannadine, 'The Context, Performance and Meaning of Ritual: The British monarchy and the "invention of tradition", c.1820–1977' in E.J. Hobsbawm and T. Ranger (eds), *The Invention of Tradition*, Cambridge, Cambridge University Press, 1983, pp. 101–64.

21 F. D'Arcy, 'Charles Bradlaugh and the English Republican Movement, 1868–1878', *Historical Journal*, 1982, vol. 25, pp. 367–83.

22 L. Colley, *Britons: Forging the nation, 1707–1837*, New Haven, CT and London, Yale University Press, 1992, ch. 5.

23 R. McKibbin, 'Class and Conventional Wisdom: The Conservative party and the "public" in inter-war Britain' in his *The Ideologies of Class: Social relations in Britain*, 1880–1950, Oxford, Oxford University Press, 1991, pp. 259–93.

CONCLUSION: TOWARDS POST-REVISIONISM

1 R. Gray, 'Class, Politics and Historical "Revisionism"', *Social History*, 1994, vol. 19, p. 220.

2 P. Joyce, *Democratic Subjects: The self and the social in nineteenth-century England*, Cambridge, Cambridge University Press, 1994; M. Poovey, *Making a Social Body: British cultural formation, 1830–1864*, Chicago, IL, University of Chicago Press, 1995.

3 D. Reid, 'Reflections on Labor History and Language' in L. Berlanstein (ed.), *Rethinking Labor History: Essays on discourse and class analysis*, Urbana, IL, University of Illinois Press, 1993, pp. 39–54.

4 J. Epstein, *Radical Expression: Political language, ritual and symbol in England, 1790–1850*, New York, Oxford University Press, 1994; J. Vernon (ed.), *Re-reading the Constitution: New narratives in the political history of England's long nineteenth century*, Cambridge, Cambridge University Press, 1996.

Bibliography

This bibliography is a guide to key works published in the last two decades. References to other standard works will be found in the endnotes and the text.

Adelman, P., *Victorian Radicalism: The middle-class experience, 1830–1914*, London, Longman, 1984.

Alexander, S., 'Women, Class and Sexual Differences in the 1830s and 1840s: Some reflections on the writing of a feminist history', *History Workshop Journal*, 1984, no. 17, pp. 125–49.

Barrow, L. and Bullock, I., *Democratic Ideas and the British Labour Movement, 1880–1914*, Cambridge, Cambridge University Press, 1996.

Behagg, C., *Politics and Production in the Early Nineteenth Century*, London, Routledge, 1990.

Belchem, J., 'Republicanism, Popular Constitutionalism and the Radical Platform in Early Nineteenth Century England', *Social History*, 1981, vol. 6, pp. 1–32.

—— *'Orator' Hunt: Henry Hunt and English working-class radicalism*, Oxford, Clarendon Press, 1985.

—— *Popular Radicalism in Nineteenth-Century Britain*, London, Macmillan, 1996.

Belchem, J. and Epstein, J., 'The Nineteenth-Century Gentleman Leader Revisited', *Social History*, 1997, vol. 22, pp. 174–93.

Bellamy, J.M. and Saville, J. (eds), *Dictionary of Labour Biography*, London, Macmillan, 1972–93, 9 vols.

Bevir, M., 'The British Social Democratic Federation, 1880–1885: From O'Brienism to Marxism', *International Review of Social History*, 1992, vol. 37, pp. 207–29.

Biagini, E.F., *Liberty, Retrenchment and Reform: Popular Liberalism in the age of Gladstone, 1860–1880*, Cambridge, Cambridge University Press, 1992.

Biagini, E.F. (ed.), *Citizenship and Community: Liberals, radicals and collective identities in the British Isles, 1865–1931*, Cambridge, Cambridge University Press, 1996.

Biagini, E.F. and Reid, A.J. (eds), *Currents of Radicalism: Popular radicalism, organised labour and party politics in Britain, 1850–1914*, Cambridge, Cambridge University Press, 1991.

Calhoun, C., *The Question of Class Struggle: Social foundations of popular radicalism during the Industrial Revolution*, Chicago, IL, University of Chicago Press, 1981.

Chase, C., *The People's Farm: English radical agrarianism, 1775–1840*, Oxford, Clarendon Press, 1988.

Claeys, M., *Machinery, Money and the Millennium: From moral economy to socialism, 1815–1860*, Cambridge, Polity Press, 1987.

—— *Citizens and Saints: Politics and anti-politics in early British socialism*, Cambridge, Cambridge University Press, 1989.

Clark, A., *The Struggle for the Breeches: Gender and the making of the British working class*, London, Rivers Oram Press, 1995.

Colley, L., *Britons: Forging the nation, 1707–1837*, New Haven, CT, and London, Yale University Press, 1992.

Colls, R. and Dodd, P. (eds), *Englishness: Politics and culture, 1880–1920*, London, Croom Helm, 1986.

Crossick, G., *An Artisan Elite in Victorian Society: Kentish London, 1840–1880*, London, Croom Helm, 1978.

Cunningham, H., 'The language of patriotism, 1750–1914', *History Workshop Journal*, 1981, no. 12, pp. 8–33.

D'Arcy, F., 'Charles Bradlaugh and the English Republican Movement, 1868–1878', *Historical Journal*, 1982, vol. 25, pp. 367–83.

Davis, J., *Reforming London: The London government problem, 1855–1900*, Oxford, Oxford University Press, 1988.

Dinwiddy, J., *Radicalism and Reform in Britain, 1780–1850*, London, Hambledon Press, 1992.

Dyck, I., *William Cobbett and Rural Popular Culture*, Cambridge, Cambridge University Press, 1992.

Eley, G., 'Edward Thompson, Social History and Political Culture: The making of a working-class public, 1780–1850' in Kaye, H. and McClelland, K. (eds), *E.P. Thompson: Critical perspectives*, London, Polity Press, 1990, pp. 12–49.

Epstein, J., *The Lion of Freedom: Feargus O'Connor and the Chartist Movement*, London, Croom Helm, 1982.

—— *Radical Expression: Political language, ritual, and symbol in England, 1790–1850*, New York, Oxford University Press, 1994.

Epstein, J. and Thompson, D. (eds), *The Chartist Experience: Studies in working-class radicalism and culture, 1830–1860*, London, Macmillan, 1982.

Feldman, D., *Englishmen and Jews: Social relations and political culture, 1840–1914*, New Haven, CT, and London, Yale University Press, 1994.

Finn, M.C., *After Chartism: Class and nation in English radical politics, 1848–1874*, Cambridge, Cambridge University Press, 1993.

Gossman, N.J. and Baylen, J.O. (eds), *Biographical Dictionary of Modern British Radicals*, Brighton, Harvester Press, 1979–88, 3 vols.

Gray, R., *The Aristocracy of Labour in Nineteenth-Century Britain, c.1850–1900*, London, Macmillan, 1981.

Green, E.H.H., *The Crisis of Conservatism: The politics, economics and ideology of the British Conservative party, 1880–1914*, London, Routledge, 1995.

Hall, C., *White, Male and Middle Class: Explorations in feminism and history*, London, Polity Press, 1992.

Hamer, D.A., *The Politics of Electoral Pressure: A study in the history of Victorian reform agitations*, Hassocks, Harvester Press, 1977.

Harling, P. and Mandler, P., 'From "Fiscal-Military" State to Laissez-Faire State, 1760–1850', *Journal of British Studies*, 1993, vol. 32, pp. 44–70.

Harrison, J.F.C., *The Second Coming: Popular Millenarianism, 1780–1850*, London, Routledge & Kegan Paul, 1979.

Hart, V., *Democracy and Distrust: Political distrust in Britain and America*, Cambridge, Cambridge University Press, 1978.

Hobsbawm, E.J., *Worlds of Labour: Further studies in the history of labour*, London, Weidenfeld & Nicolson, 1984.

Hobsbawm, E.J. and Ranger, T. (eds), *The Invention of Tradition*, Cambridge, Cambridge University Press, 1983.

Hollis, P., *Ladies Elect: Women in English local government, 1865–1914*, Oxford, Clarendon Press, 1987.

Howell, D., *British Workers and the Independent Labour Party, 1888–1906*, Manchester, Manchester University Press, 1983.

Howkins, A., *Poor Labouring Men: Rural radicalism in Norfolk, 1872–1923*, London, Routledge & Kegan Paul, 1985.

Hunt, E.H., *British Labour History, 1815–1914*, London, Weidenfeld & Nicolson, 1981.

Hunt, K., *Equivocal Feminists: The Social Democratic Federation and the woman question, 1884–1911*, Cambridge, Cambridge University Press, 1996.

Jenkins, T.A., *The Liberal Ascendancy, 1830–1886*, London, Macmillan, 1994.

Jones, G.S., *Languages of Class: Studies in English working-class history, 1832–1982*, Cambridge, Cambridge University Press, 1983.

Joyce, P., *Work, Society and Politics: The culture of the factory in later Victorian England*, Hassocks, Harvester Press, 1980.

—— *Visions of the People: Industrial England and the question of class, c.1840–1914*, Cambridge, Cambridge University Press, 1991.

—— *Democratic Subjects: The self and the social in nineteenth century England*, Cambridge, Cambridge University Press, 1994.

Kirk, N., *The Growth of Working-Class Reformism in Mid-Victorian England*, London, Croom Helm, 1985.

Lancaster, B., *Radicalism, Cooperation and Socialism: Leicester working-class politics, 1860–1906*, Leicester, Leicester University Press, 1987.

Lawrence, J., 'Popular Radicalism and the Socialist Revival in Britain', *Journal of British Studies*, 1992, vol. 31, pp. 163–86.

—— 'Class and Gender in the Making of Urban Toryism, 1880–1914', *English Historical Review*, 1993, vol. 108, pp. 628–52.

Lawrence, J. and Taylor, M. (eds), *Party, State and Society: Electoral behaviour in Britain since 1820*, London, Scolar Press, 1996.

Laybourn, K. and Reynolds, J., *Liberalism and the Rise of Labour, 1890–1918*, London, Croom Helm, 1984.

McCalman, I., *Radical Underworld: Prophets, revolutionaries and pornographers in London, 1795–1840*, Cambridge, Cambridge University Press, 1988.

McKibbin, R., *The Ideologies of Class: Social relations in Britain, 1880–1950*, Oxford, Clarendon Press, 1990.

Matthew, H.C.G., 'Rhetoric and Politics in Great Britain, 1860–1950' in Waller, P. J. (ed.), *Politics and Social Change in Britain*, Brighton, Harvester Press, 1987, pp. 34–58.

Midgely, C., *Women against Slavery: The British campaigns, 1780–1870*, London, Routledge, 1992.

Mort, F., *Dangerous Sexualities: Medico-moral politics in Britain since 1830*, London, Routledge & Kegan Paul, 1987.

Nash, D., *Secularism, Art and Freedom*, Leicester, Leicester University Press, 1992.

Newman, G., *The Rise of English Nationalism: A cultural history, 1740–1830*, New York, St Martin's Press, 1987.

O'Gorman, F., *Voters, Patrons and Parties: The unreformed electoral system of Hanoverian England, 1734–1832*, Oxford, Clarendon Press, 1989.

Parry, J.P., *The Rise and Fall of Liberal Government in Victorian Britain*, New Haven, CT, and London, Yale University Press, 1993.

Paz, D., *Popular Anti-Catholicism in Mid-Victorian England*, Stanford, CA, Stanford University Press, 1992.

Phillips, J.A., *Electoral Behaviour in Unreformed England: Plumpers, splitters and straights*, Princeton, NJ, Princeton University Press, 1982.

—— *The Great Reform Bill in the Boroughs: English electoral behaviour, 1818–1841*, Oxford, Clarendon Press, 1992.

Pickering, P.A., *Chartism and the Chartists in Manchester and Salford*, London, Macmillan, 1995.

Prest, J., *Liberty and Locality: Parliament, permissive legislation and ratepayers' democracies in the nineteenth century*, Oxford, Clarendon Press, 1990.

Price, R., *Labour in British Society: An interpretive history*, London, Croom Helm, 1986.

Prothero, I.J., *Artisans and Politics in Early Nineteenth Century London: John Gast and his times*, Folkestone, Dawson, 1979.

Pugh, M., *The Tories and the People, 1880–1935*, Oxford, Basil Blackwell, 1985.

Quinault, R., '1848 and Parliamentary Reform', *Historical Journal*, 1988, vol. 31, pp. 831–51.

—— 'The Industrial Revolution and Parliamentary Reform' in O'Brien, P. and Quinault, R. (eds), *The Industrial Revolution and British Society*, Cambridge, Cambridge University Press, 1993, pp. 183–202.

Read, D., *Peel and the Victorians*, Oxford, Basil Blackwell, 1987.

Reay, B., *The Last Rising of the Agricultural Labourers: Rural life and protest in nineteenth-century England*, Oxford, Clarendon Press, 1990.

Reed, M. and Wells, R. (eds), *Class, Conflict and Protest in the English Countryside, 1700–1880*, London, Cass, 1990.

Rendall, J. (ed.), *Equal or Different: Women's politics, 1800–1914*, Oxford, Basil Blackwell, 1987.

Richter, D., *Riotous Victorians*, Athens, OH, Ohio University Press, 1981.

Roberts, S., *Radical Politicians and Poets in Early Victorian Britain: The voices of six Chartist leaders*, Lampeter, Edwin Mellen Press, 1993.

Royle, E., *Radicals, Secularists and Republicans: Popular free thought in Britain, 1866–1915*, Manchester, Manchester University Press, 1980.

Rule, J., *The Labouring Classes in Early Industrial England, 1750–1850*, London, Longman, 1986.

Samuel, R. (ed.), *Patriotism: The making and unmaking of British national identity*, London, Routledge, 1989, 3 vols.

Savage, M., *The Dynamics of Working-Class Politics: The labour movement in Preston, 1880–1940*, Cambridge, Cambridge University Press, 1987.

Savage, M. and Miles, A., *The Remaking of the British Working Class, 1840–1940*, London, Routledge, 1994.

Saville, J., *1848: The British State and the Chartist movement*, Cambridge, Cambridge University Press, 1987.

—— *The Labour Movement in Britain: A commentary*, London, Faber & Faber, 1988.

Schwarzkopf, J., *Women in the Chartist Movement*, London, Macmillan, 1991.

Scott, J.W., *Gender and the Politics of History*, New York, Columbia University Press, 1988.

Searle, G.R., *Entrepreneurial Politics in Mid-Victorian Britain*, Oxford, Oxford University Press, 1993.

Smith, O., *The Politics of Language, 1791–1819*, Oxford, Clarendon Press, 1984.

Stafford, W., *Socialism, Radicalism and Nostalgia: Social criticism in Britain, 1775–1830*, Cambridge, Cambridge University Press, 1987.

Tanner, D., *Political Change and the Labour Party, 1900–1918*, Cambridge, Cambridge University Press, 1990.

Taylor, B., *Eve and the New Jerusalem: Socialism and feminism in the nineteenth century*, London, Virago, 1983.

Taylor, M., 'John Bull and the Iconography of Public Opinion in England, c.1712–1929', *Past and Present*, 1992, no. 134, pp. 93–128.

—— *The Decline of British Radicalism, 1847–1860*, Oxford, Clarendon Press, 1995.

—— 'Rethinking the Chartists: Searching for synthesis in the historiography of Chartism', *Historical Journal*, 1996, vol. 39, pp. 479–95.

Taylor, P., *Popular Politics in Industrial Britain: Bolton, 1825–1850*, Keele, Ryburn Publishing, 1995.

Thane, P., 'The Working Class and State "Welfare" in Britain, 1880–1914', *Historical Journal*, 1984, vol. 27, pp. 877–900.

Tholfsen, T.R., *Working-Class Radicalism in Mid-Victorian England*, London, Croom Helm, 1977.

Thompson, D., *The Chartists: Popular politics in the Industrial Revolution*, London, Temple Smith, 1984.

—— *Outsiders: Class, gender and nation*, London, Verso, 1993.

Thompson, N., *The People's Science: The popular political economy of exploitation and crisis, 1816–1834*, Cambridge, Cambridge University Press, 1984.

—— *The Market and its Critics: Socialist political economy in nineteenth-century Britain*, London, Routledge, 1988.

Vernon, J., *Politics and the People: A study in English political culture, c.1815–1867*, Cambridge, Cambridge University Press, 1993.

—— (ed.), *Re-reading the Constitution: New narratives in the political history of England's long nineteenth century*, Cambridge, Cambridge University Press, 1996.

Wahrman, D., *Imagining the Middle Class: The political representation of class in Britain, c.1780–1840*, Cambridge, Cambridge University Press, 1995.

Walkowitz, J., *City of Dreadful Delight: Narratives of sexual danger in late Victorian London*, London, Virago, 1992.

Ward, P., *The Red Flag and the Union Jack*, forthcoming, 1998.

Waters, C., *British Socialists and the Politics of Popular Culture*, Manchester, Manchester University Press, 1990.

Weaver, S., *John Fielden and the Politics of Popular Radicalism, 1832–1847*, Oxford, Clarendon Press, 1987.

Winstanley, M., 'Oldham Radicalism and the Origins of Popular Radicalism, 1830–1852', *Historical Journal*, 1993, vol. 36, pp. 619–43.

Wolffe, J., *The Protestant Crusade in Great Britain, 1829–1860*, Oxford, Clarendon Press, 1991.

Wright, D.G., *Popular Radicalism: The working-class experience, 1780–1880*, London, Longman, 1988.

Yeo, E., 'Culture and Constraint in Working-Class Movements, 1830–1855' in Yeo, E. and Yeo, S. (eds), *Popular Culture and Class Conflict, 1590–1914: Explorations in the history of labour and leisure*, Brighton, Harvester Press, 1981, pp. 115–86.

—— 'Christianity in Chartist Struggle, 1836–1842', *Past and Present*, 1981, no. 91, pp. 109–39.

Yeo, S., 'A New Life: The religion of socialism in Britain, 1883–1896', *History Workshop Journal*, 1977, no. 4., pp. 5–56.

Index